THE PERSONAL GROWTH STUDY GUIDES

FULFILLMENT

The Adventure of Life Worth Living

LARRY RICHARDS

THOMAS NELSON PUBLISHERS
Nashville • Atlanta • London • Vancouver

ISBN 0-7852-1145-4

Printed in the United States of America
1 2 3 4 5 6 — 00 99 98 97 96

CONTENTS

RelationshipBuilding
Growing Wiser in Living with Others

SpiritBuilding
Growing Toward Total Wholeness

RelationshipBuilding
Growing Wiser in Living with Others

PART THREE: *DAILY STEPS*

FaithBuilding
Growing Closer to God

SpiritBuilding
Growing Toward Total Wholeness

RelationshipBuilding
Growing Wiser in Living with Others

PREFACE

What Is Personal Growth?

The idea behind the **Personal Growth™ Study Guide** series of books is that we grow in three dimensions. We grow internally [CharacterBuilding]. We grow in and through our relationship with God [FaithBuilding]. And we grow in and through our relationship with others [RelationshipBuilding].

Each **Personal Growth™ Study Guide** book explores a significant aspect of human life in terms of character building, faith building, and relationship building. The first four books, available now in your Christian bookstore or from the publisher, explore Intimacy, Holiness, Fulfillment, and Forgiveness. Look for additional titles, coming soon.

There is also a **Personal Growth™ Study Bible.** This vital study and devotional Bible identifies and comments on key passages throughout God's Word that help us develop Christian character, Christian faith, and Christian interpersonal relationships. The quotes at the end of the chapters are insights taken from the **Personal Growth™ Study Bible.**

If you want to build your life on God's Word, don't miss getting this practical and invaluable Bible, available NOW.

Personal Growth™ Study Guide Books

Personal Growth™ Study Guide books are topical. They provide in-depth insights into life's most significant issues. Their focus is illustrated by these first four compelling titles:

Intimacy: The secrets of loving and being loved
Forgiveness: The gift that heals and sets free
Holiness: The blessings of the good life
Fulfillment: The adventure of life worth living

Personal Growth™ Study Guide books are rooted in Scripture, and grow out of the author's conviction that God's Word supplies all the guidance we need. These fresh, easy-to-read books provide easy access to biblical principles that can revolutionize our lives.

How to Use Personal Growth™ Study Guide Books

Personal Growth™ Study Guide books are written for your personal enrichment. One way to use these books is to read them in your own home. Questions at the end of each chapter will help you apply principles to your life, while quotes from the **Personal Growth™ Study Bible** encourage meditation.

Personal Growth™ Study Guide books are also ideal for study groups. There's a Teaching Plan section at the back of each book designed to stimulate shared exploration of the life-changing truths developed in each chapter. **Personal Growth™ Study Guide** book studies can add a dynamic dimension to your Sunday school class, home Bible study, vacation Bible school, or other group meetings. While the **Personal Growth™ Study Guides** were designed with the **Personal Growth™ Study Bible** in mind, you may use them with any Bible and get full benefit from them!

The NEW Personal Growth™ Study Bible

Personal Growth™ Study Guide books are intimately linked to the new **Personal Growth™ Study Bible.** Each book develops in a single study one of the many essential Personal Growth themes identified in the study Bible. This unique study Bible explores the whole Word of God, highlights principles that will help believers understand how to grow in a personal relationship with God and relationships with others, and shows how to develop a strong, godly character. Unlike other study Bibles, which concentrate on providing information about the text, the **Personal Growth™ Study Bible** concentrates on identifying the Personal Growth principles in Scripture and applying these principles daily. **The Personal Growth™ Study Bible** points to key texts and how to understand them, and then leads to God's goal of transformation!

About the Author

The **Personal Growth™ Study Bible** and **Personal Growth™ Study Guide** books are the work of Dr. Larry Richards. Larry has written over 140 books in his thirty-year ministry. His works include Christian Education textbooks which have been translated into twenty-two languages and are used in leading Bible colleges and seminaries throughout the world. Larry is the author of the *Expository Dictionary of Bible Words*, which explores the Greek and Hebrew roots of Scripture, the *Revell Bible Dictionary*, and many other works on Scripture.

Most important to Larry are the many devotional and study books he's written which speak to the hearts of believers. **The Personal Growth**™ **Study Bible** and **Personal Growth**™ **Study Guide** books are the culmination of Larry's thirty years of studying and teaching God's Word.

ON OUR OWN

Nathaniel was home again. It was exciting to be back in Africa after studying in America. It was especially exciting not only to be the pastor of his community's church, but also to be a landowner.

It hadn't been easy. But the Lord had provided money so he and his wife could buy a property from a friend of theirs. There had been many difficulties, but at last everything was done. They had the money from the bank. They had paid their friend. The property was transferred. They were happy.

But then they wanted to fence the plot. First, of course, they had to know the exact boundary marks. Nathaniel asked all the people whose plots touched on theirs to show him the end of their property. They all did, and their plots ended exactly where the person who sold them the plot said. Except for one neighbor. This one person claimed that his parcel extended ½ acre into Nathaniel's new property.

So they all agreed to call the town surveyor. The surveyor came and showed the correct points. But the neighbor did not believe them. Nathaniel called three different surveyors on different dates. But the neighbor would not believe any of them. Then Nathaniel summoned the village elders. These people had been there during the time the land was first divided. The elders all agreed with Nathaniel, but the neighbor became more stubborn.

Nathaniel writes, "through all these processes, my patience was waning. Frustration and anger set in. I became so *angry!* God forgive me, what made me angry was that both of us were believers. More than that, I was a pastor, he and his family were members of our church, and what I considered mature believers. We were supposed to be different, a light and salt to the world, but here, obviously, we were not."

Nathaniel's humanness took hold of him, and he began preaching vindictive messages. He preached on honesty, justice, and truthfulness. But he was not preaching. He was fighting, using the right tool—God's Word—but for the wrong motive.

Karen was feeling frustrated, too. She was a member of a small Bible study group, and she'd had such hopes when she joined it. Karen, like most of us, had many personal needs she hoped the others would meet. She'd tried so hard to help the others, hoping desperately that they'd be good to her in return. But they hadn't lived up to her expectations. All her efforts seemed to produce nothing. So as she thought about the group one week she was feeling especially dissatisfied and cheated.

Liz was another person who was frustrated. Some eighteen years before she had found Christ outside the church in which she'd been brought up. Although her new faith brought her joy, Liz suddenly found herself in a difficult struggle. Each family member took personal offense at her decision. Her father, who had modeled Christ to her all her life, was especially distraught. Liz was shocked at his reaction of rage. She felt more and more persecuted and attacked for loving the God she thought her father raised her to love, while he thought her talk of a new and deeply personal relationship with Jesus was simply arrogant.

As Liz grew as a Christian she could see that the church in which she was raised had teachings that ran counter to the Word of God. The trouble was that as she identified what she felt was error, she could feel herself growing judgmental.

It all came to a head when one of her sisters invited her to a christening. Athough Liz was the oldest sister and the one her family still turned to when they hurt, Liz wasn't asked to be godmother to the child. That hurt. And it hurt too, sitting in the pew, feeling both frustrated and angry as she thought about the false doctrines that held her family in bondage. How could they continue in a church that promoted such false doctrines?

Jesus' Hillside Teachings

One day Jesus stood on a hillside and shocked the crowds. People very much like Nathaniel and Karen and Liz were there. There are people like these three in every group, in every church, in every family. Angry people, frustrated people, hurting and judgmental people. People who try to make their way through life as best they can, but who all too often stumble into troubles they never expected.

That day on a hillside in Galilee Jesus shocked His listeners by presenting a totally unexpected way out of our human difficulties. A way that is recorded in Matthew 5 through 7, in what we know as Jesus' Sermon on the Mount. Jesus' way was unexpected because it runs counter to how we human beings tend to approach life on our own.

For instance, Jesus spoke of the fulfillment, the blessing, that comes to those who are "poor in spirit." On our own we draw back from poverty of any kind. We want to be rich: rich in money, rich in intelligence, rich in looks and social status.

Jesus spoke of the fulfillment, the blessing, that comes to those who "mourn." On our own we make every effort to avoid sorrows. We want our life to be filled: filled with friends and loved ones, filled with excitement, filled with accomplishment.

Jesus spoke of fulfillment in a way that runs counter to how we human beings approach life on our own.

Jesus spoke of the fulfillment, the blessing, that comes to those who are "persecuted for righteousness." On our own we avoid persecution. We want to be liked, to be admired, to be listened to, to influence others to see and do things our way.

It's no wonder then that those who first heard Jesus' Sermon on the Mount drew back, amazed. What was Jesus talking about? How could blessing, how could fulfillment, be found in the things that Jesus seemed to promote? Could Jesus' way, so drastically different from our own way, possibly offer what human beings search for but never seem to find?

While Jesus' first listeners doubted, Nathaniel and Karen and Liz all learned to believe. It happened this past summer, as they prepared for a course on the life of Christ, with special emphasis on Jesus' teachings on personal relationships. Before the course began each was to read the books of Matthew and Luke through, select one passage on personal relationships that seemed especially significant, and apply that passage to his or her life. Here, in their own words, is what happened when they left their own way and took a path that Jesus pointed out in His unlikely hillside sermon, given that long-ago day.

Back in Africa, in the grip of anger and frustration, Nathaniel read Matthew 5:21–26. That day on the hillside Jesus had taught, "You have heard that it was said to those of old, *'You shall not murder,* and whosoever murders will be in danger of judgment.' But I say to you that whoever is angry with his brother without a cause shall be in danger of the judgment . . . . Therefore if you bring your gift to the altar, and there remember that your brother has something against you, leave your gift there before the altar, and go your way. First be reconciled to your brother, and then come and offer your gift." Nathaniel tells us his story.

> *That day the Lord took hold of my heart. "First be reconciled to your brother, and then come and offer your gift." I knew that God was speaking to me in that passage; that He was not pleased with my worship or my service to Him when in my heart, I was constantly angry with my brother.*
>
> *Immediately I went to him. I asked for forgiveness from him and from God. When he saw what I did, he asked forgiveness also. We forgave each other. What a peaceful day that was!*
>
> *Amazingly, a few days later, my neighbor came to my house with a solution to the plot issue. We took the disputed parcel and divided it evenly. We were reconciled. Our relationship was repaired, our fellowship grew, and our worship of God became whole.*

It was through a different passage, Matthew 11:16–19, that God spoke to Karen. She read about the people who criticized John the Baptist for his austere life, and then when Jesus came enjoying social times with others, they criticized Him too. She writes,

> *Here is a picture of a people who are never satisfied. They scheme and manipulate others for their selfish ends, yet nobody can ever provide what they really want.*
>
> *I was humbled to discover that this was an accurate description of many of my relationships. I often interact with people in ways that are designed to manipulate them to somehow meet my own needs. When they do not live up to these expectations, I become dissatisfied and feel cheated.*
>
> *The evening after God revealed this to me, I had my small*

group Bible study. I prayed that God would provide an opportunity to somehow apply the principles He was teaching me. I felt that this was a perfect opportunity because I had recently been feeling that the group had not been meeting my needs. I was not sure what that prayer would bring about, but I arrived at that evening's meeting with a different attitude. I went with a heart that was truly looking for opportunities to encourage, no matter what the cost to myself.

What happened that night was not a major turning point in my life. However, I found many opportunities to simply encourage, to be vulnerable at times when I believed my experiences would be of benefit to another, and I did not hold back as I often do. I did not wait for others to meet my needs but actively searched out ways to become more deeply involved in their lives, regardless of their response. As a result, I left the meeting that night knowing that I had touched others' lives in a meaningful way and that I had truly offered a

> The satisfaction had come in giving myself, not in receiving.

piece of myself. I felt more committed to and invested in their lives. And I felt more satisfied than I had in a long time. The satisfaction had come in giving myself, not in receiving.

A week later, one of the girls even told me that she had thought all week about one of the examples I had shared with her that night and that those words had significantly changed her walk with God. I was filled with gratitude that God had used me in such a way, a way that would not have been possible if I had been pursuing my own ends.

The words that spoke to Liz came from the Sermon on the Mount. Jesus had said, "And why do you look at the speck in your brother's eye, but do not consider the plank in your own eye? Or how can you say to your brother, 'Let me remove the speck from your eye'; and look, a plank is in your own eye? Hypocrite! First remove the plank from your own eye, and then you will see clearly to remove the speck from your brother's eye" (Matt. 7:3–5).

Liz shares what this passage meant to her. "It was easy for me to judge my family for choosing to remain in a church that has teachings that run counter to the Word of God, when they have all professed to know Him as their personal Lord and Savior. It wasn't easy to look at the attitude of my heart that they could see all too well. I felt the Lord ripping out of me my demanding spirit, and teaching me to rest quietly in Him and obey Him by acting in love when my family persecutes me."

Shortly after reading and thinking about this passage Liz was invited to another christening. She writes,

> I was thankful for this new occasion where I could show love to my family by being present at the ceremony, supporting my brother and his wife as they dedicated their little girl to the Lord. My heart felt right this time; I went with the energy to "love" my family instead of "judge" them. I realize they are not my enemies, but the doctrines that hold them in bondage are the enemies. I chose to pray, but not in an arrogant manner this time. Through God's grace I was able to separate the issues that cause me to react to the persecution. I chose to work on the plank in my own eye in my pride and arrogance at not being chosen as godmother, rather than focus on the speck in my family's eye. There was still some pain at the ceremony, but this time it wasn't self-centered, and I tasted of the pain that Jesus must have felt as He wept for Jerusalem. My heart shifted to other-centered love as I focused on their needs rather than my own hurt.

Fulfillment

The *American Heritage Encyclopedic Dictionary* defines "fulfillment" as the "satisfaction gained from fully realizing one's personal aims or potential." The problem is that often our personal aims are inappropriate. When this is the case, gaining those aims won't bring satisfaction.

Nathaniel wanted to establish his right to the land he had purchased. With the surveyors, the neighbors, and the village elders on his side, he might have gone ahead and fenced the land he rightfully owned. But if he had, he would have won the undying hostility of a Christian brother, and would surely have driven him from the church he pastored.

Karen wanted to establish herself and her needs as the central focus of a small Bible study group she was a part of. But what if they had all focused on her? Karen would have lost the

chance to be *self-less,* and so to be a channel through whom
God ministered to the others.

Liz wanted to confront her family members with their error
and make them abandon the church she had left. Their response
to the pressure they felt from her was to resist and to strike back
at the implied criticism of their convictions. Her effort to control
them and their beliefs backfired, and it was only when she gave
up judging them that Christ's love began to show through.

Each of these, Nathaniel, Karen, and Liz, had tried to find
fulfillment on his or her own. Then God suddenly showed
them His way. Each took that way, and then each one began to
find what each of us is really looking for. A fulfillment that is
rooted, not in achieving our own personal ends, but the ends
that God has for us as His children.

That's what this book is all about. Fulfillment. The
fulfillment you and I as God's children can find in achieving His
ends for us and in realizing the potential we have in Christ.

Our exploration, like this book, will be divided into three
parts. First, we'll look at humankind's ideas about the ends
that can provide us with satisfaction—and discover why they
can never meet our heart's deepest needs. These studies are in
Chapters two through five. Second, we'll look at the radical
teachings of God's Word about the surprising ends that, as
we achieve them, will bring fulfillment. These studies are in
Chapters six through nine. Third, we'll explore specific,
practical, daily steps that you and I can take to achieve our
potential as Christians. We'll learn just how to find the
fulfillment, the blessing, that Jesus promises to those who
follow Him. These studies are in Chapters ten through thirteen.

Nathaniel, Karen, and Liz have all begun to experience the
difference that following Jesus' radical approach to life can make.
Come with them, and let's experience that difference ourselves!

FOR REFLECTION

1. Each of the people we met in this chapter experienced
frustrations. Can you identify one or two frustrations you face right
now?

_____

_____

2. The dictionary defines fulfillment as "satisfaction gained from fully realizing one's personal aims or potential." List two or three areas where you expect to find fulfillment.

_____

_____

Before reading the next chapter, meditate on these thoughts on Luke 19:1–9 from the Personal Growth™ Study Bible.

They say there are no miracles today. If only Jesus were still giving sight to the blind, they say, many more would believe. But the story of Zacchaeus, which follows this incident, reminds us that God is performing miracles here and now.

Zacchaeus was a chief tax collector. He made his money by bidding for the right to collect taxes, and then extorting more money than he should have. No wonder he was despised as a "sinner." But after Zacchaeus met Jesus, he stood up and announced that he was giving half his goods to the poor, and restoring fourfold anything he had obtained by fraud. The blind beggar received physical sight. But the inner transformation of Zacchaeus was even more spectacular.

Eager to see a miracle? Look around at those whose lives Jesus even now transforms.

LIFE WOULD BE BETTER IF...

We've just come back from Seattle, where the papers were filled with stories of Bill Gates, Microsoft's multibillionaire. A friend took us on a boat ride on Lake Washington, and we saw the scar in the hillside where excavators and builders have been at work for several years now constructing Gates a multifloored residence with a garage large enough for over a hundred limousines.

My friend's granddaughter works for Microsoft, and everything he related about the company suggests that Gates's management style is creative and comfortable for workers. He's provided sports facilities and given employees freedom to work at their own time and pace. Just get the work done, contribute to the team and the bottom line, and no other questions are asked.

The effectiveness of Gates's management style seems to be reflected in the skillful introduction of Microsoft's *Windows 95*. All across the country computer owners waited expectantly, primed by articles in every PC magazine, by TV reports, and by millions of CD advance samplers. When the day came, reporters crowded into press conferences, while eager buyers lined up at midnight to be one of the first to own *Windows 95*. Meanwhile, the few reporters who cared couldn't even find the location where IBM was to introduce a new operating system that may have more potential impact on the industry than *Windows 95*. Gates's promotional crew had done it right! And Gates himself was interviewed on prime time show after show and idolized as the genius with all the answers.

In many ways Bill Gates reminds me of Solomon, who was also rich, an effective organizer and administrator, and an enthusiastic builder. Solomon was also an entrepreneur, whose skill in doing business brought him a personal income that exceeded three billion dollars [$3,000,000,000] a year (see 2 Chr.

9:13), not counting taxes levied on his nation! As in the case of Bill Gates, people came from all over the world to interview Solomon, and listened in awe to whatever he had to say.

If Only . . . .

I suspect that many of us have wondered what life would be like if we had only a few of the things Gates and Solomon have enjoyed. We wouldn't even ask for all of them. But I'm quite sure most of us would say that our life would improve if we had some of the things these men seem to possess. For instance, take this little quiz, and see what *you* think. Surely your life could be better, couldn't it?

Check any item that reflects what you really believe would make your life better.

My life would be better:	Definitely!	Possibly?	No.
1. If I had $5,000,000	_____	_____	_____
2. If I was better educated	_____	_____	_____
3. If people appreciated me	_____	_____	_____
4. If my health improved	_____	_____	_____
5. If I was in charge	_____	_____	_____
6. If my spouse put me first	_____	_____	_____
7. If my needs were considered	_____	_____	_____
8. If my opinion counted	_____	_____	_____
9. If I was famous	_____	_____	_____
10. If I had a big house	_____	_____	_____
11. If I had my own business	_____	_____	_____
12. If I had unlimited sex	_____	_____	_____
13. If I had a new car	_____	_____	_____

My life would be better:	Definitely!	Possibly?	No.
14. If I had achieved my goals	_____	_____	_____
15. If my family appreciated me	_____	_____	_____
16. If I had built a business	_____	_____	_____
17. If people looked up to me	_____	_____	_____
18. If my parents had loved me	_____	_____	_____
19. If I were smarter	_____	_____	_____
20. If I had friends who cared	_____	_____	_____

Now, I don't know how you responded to any of these items. You might have checked "Definitely!" on each item. You might even be right; possibly you would be better off if you had every one of the things on this list.

But in a way, "better off" begs the question. You see, this is a book about fulfillment. So the way we really should pose the question is, *"Would I be fulfilled* if. . . ?"

To check that out we'd have to ask a person like Bill Gates, who seems to have it all. Or perhaps we could ask Solomon. Certainly Solomon had everything on that list. Did Solomon have $5,000,000? Yes, and much, much more. Was Solomon well-educated? Oh, yes. He was a poet and writer of proverbs, and even worked out classification systems for studying plants and animals (1 Kin. 4:33). And people really appreciated Solomon. They were awed by his judicial decisions and thankful for the era of peace that existed during his entire forty-year reign.

As far as we know Solomon enjoyed good health throughout his long life, and as far as being "in charge" is concerned, Solomon was an autocratic ruler whose word was law.

Solomon had many wives, and there's no doubt that while Solomon seemed to be considerate of his wives, he and they clearly put Solomon first. In fact, everyone was eager to please Solomon and to meet any needs he might have. Did Solomon's opinion count? In a way, his was the *only* opinion that counted. And fame? People traveled to Jerusalem from all over the world to see Solomon and his fabulous kingdom and to listen to his wisdom.

Unlimited sex? Why, Solomon had access to a thousand sexual partners, 700 wives and 300 concubines.

A big house? Solomon's, like the future home of Bill Gates, took thirteen years to build, and incorporated the best his era had to offer.

His own business? Solomon not only became the middleman in a lucrative trade in horses and chariots, but he also was the only Israelite king to establish sea trade with Africa. Solomon was even an industrialist, with copper mines and a copper smelter that produced metal he sold throughout the region.

It's hard to imagine Solomon taking much time off to vacation. But he surely could afford the greatest luxury his age afforded.

While Solomon couldn't buy a car, the Bible tells us he had 1,400 chariots stationed around the nation and in Jerusalem.

Solomon achieved his goals, built businesses, was looked up to. Solomon certainly was loved by his mother Bathsheba, and was chosen by his father David to succeed him as Israel's king. So Solomon, surely the wisest man of his age and possibly of all time, had it all.

But as Solomon neared the end of his life, he felt completely *unfulfilled*.

The Book of Ecclesiastes

The introduction to the Book of Ecclesiastes says it was written by "the Preacher, the son of David, king in Jerusalem." Jewish and Christian scholars have traditionally held that Solomon wrote this book in his old age.

Solomon launched his reign in a spirit of humility and piety. He asked God for an understanding heart, that he might lead God's people wisely (1 Kin. 3:9). His request pleased God, and Solomon was not only given wisdom but also blessed with long life, riches, and honor. During the early and middle years of Solomon's reign he and his nation prospered. He built the Jerusalem temple and his own magnificent palace, reorganized the government, fortified border cities, strengthened the military, and aggressively pursued his various business interests. All this time Solomon remained committed to the Lord, and knew nothing but success.

But for all his wisdom Solomon made one serious mistake. Solomon's peacetime strategy involved maintaining a strong military, but the king relied on treaties worked out with both major and minor world powers. However, it was common in that age to cement a treaty by marriage. Thus Solomon found himself married to a number of pagan women, each of whom wanted to continue to worship her own national deity. To please his wives Solomon not only permitted them to practice their religion, but also constructed shrines for their deities.

The trouble was, in his later years Solomon was moved by his passion for these women to join them in their shrines. As God's Law had warned, the foreign wives turned his heart away from the Lord (1 Kin. 11:2).

At first Solomon may not have noticed any difference. But as the months and years passed life began to lose its meaning for the king. Finally Solomon, the wisest of men, began to wonder if life held any meaning at all.

As his doubts grew, Solomon set himself a task. He would use the great intellect that God had given him, and set out on a search for life's meaning. Solomon would refuse himself no experience, taste every pleasure, travel every road that seemed to promise an answer. And Solomon would record the results of his research.

Like any competent researcher, Solomon carefully established rules for his study. Those rules are stated in Ecclesiastes 1:13. "I set my heart to seek and search out by wisdom concerning all that is done under heaven."

"I set my heart." This would become a consuming task for Solomon. It wasn't a hobby he would engage in when there was spare time. Solomon would concentrate on this project and give it his best.

"To seek and search out by wisdom." Solomon's great strength was the intellect which God had provided. So Solomon would use his powers of observation and of reasoning. He would taste, test, explore, examine, and critique. Then he would measure and reach his conclusions. This reliance by Solomon on his own mental capacity is emphasized, as seven times in this book Solomon writes of "communing with [his own] heart."

"All that is done." Solomon would rule nothing out. There was no human experience that Solomon would not probe. He would look at everything human beings can accomplish, exercise every human power and test every limitation of our life here on earth.

"Under heaven." This is perhaps the most important limitation Solomon placed on his search for meaning. Solomon would look for life's meaning in the experiences of life here and now. Solomon would not turn to revelation for information, but would rely entirely on data he could gather "under the sun." In fact this is the most emphasized of all Solomon's rules. No less than twenty-nine times in this book does Solomon say that his research and his conclusions are based on "what is done under the sun." God had spoken to Solomon twice in his life, and the great king had God's Word to guide him. But for this study, for this great experiment, Solomon consciously ruled out what God had said or might say. Solomon would approach life like a man on his own. In that way Solomon would find out if anything in this life can provide a sense of fulfillment to a man who lives it on his own, without a guiding Word from the Lord.

Can anything in life provide a sense of fulfillment to a man who lives it on his own, without a guiding word from the Lord?

And what conclusion did Solomon reach?

Remember, Solomon had everything that we sometimes think we need. But despite this, after years of unmatched success and unregulated self-indulgence, Solomon was close to despair. His treatise on life's meaning opens with the words "'Vanity of vanities,' says the Preacher; 'Vanity of vanities, all is vanity.'"

The word translated "vanity" might better be rendered in modern English as "empty," or "meaningless." What Solomon is telling us is that life on our own, even if, like him, we should have it all, is totally, utterly, empty and meaningless.

There is no way that human beings can possibly find fulfillment apart from God. And, even with God in our lives, unless we adopt His values and take His approach to living, our lives will remain empty and meaningless.

That's hard for us to understand at first. So we need to take a look together at Solomon's reasoning and see his insights reflected in the experience of the friends we met in the first chapter: Nathaniel, Karen, and Liz. Once Solomon has helped us think about human attempts to find meaning in life, we'll be able to go on, and discover how adopting God's values can turn our lives around.

There is no way that human beings can possibly find fulfillment apart from God.

In fact, adopting God's values can provide what each of us, deep down, yearns for. A fulfilling and a truly satisfying life.

FOR REFLECTION

1. Take the twenty-question quiz provided in the chapter. How many of the things listed do you now have, or have you ever had? How many do you believe would make your life better if you did have them?

_____

_____

_____

2. Read Ecclesiastes 1:1–11. Why do you suppose Solomon, who had it all, seems so discouraged?

_____

_____

_____

3. What is the most meaningful thing in your life right now? What does it provide for you? Do you sense that it can provide you with satisfaction and fulfillment?

_____

_____

_____

Before reading the next chapter, meditate on this article on Colossians 3:5–14 from the Personal Growth™ Study Bible.

Today the phrase, "the beautiful people," brings to mind the wealthy and the well-dressed, featured in slick magazines and mentioned endlessly in the tabloids. The ugly are the commoners, a little overweight, with empty checking accounts, frayed furniture, and too many children to be able to spend money on stylish clothing for themselves.

Of course, if we ignore external appearances and measure beauty by character, our idea of the beautiful will change dramatically. The ugly will be the angry, the malicious, the profane, and the filthy. And the beautiful will be the tender, the kind, the humble, the meek, the longsuffering, the patient and the forgiving. Many who are common in the eyes of the world are beautiful in the eyes of the Lord.

One way we judge our maturity as Christians is by seeing the kind of person we're attracted to. Do we yearn to be accepted by the beautiful people of this world? Or do we take delight in the companionship of ordinary people who live beautiful lives?

A LIFESTYLE OF THE RICH AND FAMOUS?

I suspect that most of us have wondered what our lives would be like if we had enough money to do anything we want. Would we travel? Build a new home? Collect new cars? Tour the nation's best restaurants? Take a ninety-day cruise? Or perhaps we'd go back to college and get an advanced degree. Or start a business. Or buy a country place, and take pleasure in landscaping and rebuilding it. Perhaps we'd have time to write that book we always wanted to write, or learn to paint pictures or play a musical instrument. There's so much we could accomplish, if only we had the money and the time.

Here in Florida, as in many other states, a person can do more than dream of having millions. He or she can drop into a store and buy a $1 ticket that any given week might win at least $7 million dollars! And, if the jackpot isn't claimed and rolls over, the winning ticket may be worth $15 million, or $24 million, or more!

Of course, if $7 million doesn't impress us, we can always go back to Solomon. Solomon's annual income of some $3 billion dollars in gold makes most of our movie and sports and Lotto millionaires look poor in comparison. Especially when you consider that you could buy a lot more for the equivalent of a dollar in Solomon's time.

Not that Solomon didn't have expenses. He not only built an expensive palace, but the daily provisions he provided for government officials described in 1 Kings 4:20–23 would have fed between 4,000 and 5,000 people! Of course Solomon, like modern politicians, probably used tax money to support the bureaucracy, and didn't touch his personal funds.

Yet when you boil it all down, it's clear that Solomon had enough money to buy everything and anything he wanted. In fact, if we read Solomon's report of his search for meaning in life, we discover that Solomon **did** buy anything and everything he wanted. He indulged himself totally. That was part of his strategy for looking for fulfillment in the things human beings can do in this world. But when Solomon had indulged himself completely, he made a discouraging discovery.

The Weaknesses of Wealth

Solomon had all the money he needed to indulge every inclination. If Solomon had used his money for sinful pleasures, we might expect him to be disappointed. But Solomon didn't become a drunk or a glutton, or spend his money on prostitutes. Instead Solomon used his money in ways that let him develop his higher potentials. He had so much wealth he could test his creative and artistic limits, and see just how much he might achieve. In Chapter 2 of Ecclesiastes Solomon describes some of the things he did with his money. He says,

> I searched in my heart *how* to gratify my flesh with wine, while guiding my heart with wisdom, and how to lay hold on folly, till I might see what was good for the sons of men to do under heaven all the days of their lives.
>
> I made my works great, I built myself houses, and planted myself vineyards. I made myself gardens and orchards, and I planted all kinds of fruit trees in them.
>
> I made myself water pools from which to water the growing trees of the grove. I acquired male and female servants, and had servants born in my house. Yes, I had greater possessions of herds and flocks than all who were in Jerusalem before me.
>
> I also gathered for myself silver and gold and the special treasures of kings and of the provinces. I acquired male and female singers, the delights of the sons of men, and musical instruments of all kinds.
>
> So I became great and excelled more than all who were before me in Jerusalem. Also my wisdom remained with me.
>
> Whatever my eyes desired I did not keep from them. I did not withhold my heart from any pleasure, for my heart rejoiced in all my labor.

Ecclesiastes 2:3–10

During the exciting days of creation Solomon's heart seems to have beat faster with enthusiasm. But when he had done everything, and paused to evaluate, Solomon says, "I looked on all the works that my hands had done and on the labor in which I had toiled; and indeed all was vanity and grasping for the wind" (2:11). Ultimately, it was all meaningless.

But why?

What was it that convinced Solomon that using his money to enable him to achieve great things was meaningless? After all, Solomon hadn't turned into a drunk or glutton. He'd turned into one of the world's most accomplished builders and architects. Solomon used his money to develop his talent, to design beautiful things, to construct fine buildings. Psychologists call this self-actualization—becoming and being all one can be. And they tell us that this kind of effort provides the deepest possible satisfaction.

But despite Solomon's wise use of his money, and indulging himself in truly fitting ways, when Solomon reviewed his life he was forced to conclude that what he'd done was meaningless.

> When Solomon reviewed his life he was forced to conclude that what he'd done was meaningless.

Why? Solomon gives us reasons.

Death awaits all (2:15). Solomon had spent his life wisely, using his wealth to accomplish positive ends. But then Solomon compared his choices in life with those made by a "fool." The word for "fool" here is one of several in Hebrew that are translated by our English word. The Hebrew words have something in common. None looks at foolishness from an intellectual point of view. Each looks at foolishness from a moral point of view. The "fool" of the Bible is morally deficient, not mentally challenged.

Solomon had used his wealth in an appropriate way to reach morally higher ends and satisfy morally appropriate needs. But in the final analysis Solomon was forced to a strange conclusion. Ultimately there was no difference between Solomon and a "fool" who would use his wealth in an immoral or base way.

Both die.

What happens to the fool happens to Solomon!

So Solomon laments, "there is no more remembrance of the wise than of the fool forever, since all that now is will be forgotten in the days to come. And how does a wise man die? As the fool!" (2:16).

We can't take it with us (2:18). There was another thing that bothered Solomon. He had amassed great wealth, and used that wealth to build and to create. But as Solomon thought about death, he realized that "I must leave it to the man who will come after me."

The problem here is that Solomon had no idea what kind of person the individual who inherited what Solomon would leave might be. "Who knows whether he will be wise or a fool? Yet he will rule over all my labor in which I toiled and in which I have shown myself wise under the sun" (2:19). If the heir is wise, what Solomon has built might remain for a generation or two. But if the heir is foolish, or if the heir's successor is foolish, all Solomon's accomplishments might fade and be gone within a generation.

Nothing that Solomon has worked for has any permanent value. With the passage of time Solomon's great accomplishments will crumble into the dust, to be picked over a millennium later by archaeologists who study the remains, but who will never see Solomon's architectural wonders standing in all their original beauty. Considering this, Solomon is struck by the meaninglessness of everything he has done. He has worked so hard, and created so much beauty. But for what? For nothing!

It isn't fair (2:21). As Solomon contemplates leaving behind everything he used his wealth to create, he is overwhelmed with a sense of unfairness. "For there is a man whose labor is with wisdom, knowledge, and skill; yet he must leave his heritage to a man who has not labored for it."

Wise or foolish, Solomon's heir doesn't deserve to inherit what *Solomon* has worked so hard to accomplish. "This also is vanity," Solomon says, and goes on, "For what has man for all his labor, and for the striving of his heart with which he has toiled under the sun?" (2:22). Solomon did all the work, but will he be the one to benefit from it? He must die and leave everything behind, to a person who did nothing to earn what Solomon will leave. Contemplating the unfairness of it all, Solomon is again overwhelmed with a sense of life's meaninglessness.

It is striking that Solomon has spent his life and his fortune developing the gifts God gave him. Yet, rather than finding satisfaction, Solomon has determined that life is more meaningless than ever.

What Happened to All That Gold?

History illustrates the very points that so troubled Solomon. For a long time some scholars derided the Bible's report of Solomon's vast wealth, and scoffed at the idea that anyone in the ancient world could have collected so much gold.

This is especially true of the Bible's description of the temple Solomon built. According to the text, every inner and outer surface was covered with gold (see 1 Kin. 5—7). The key furnishings were of solid gold. Add to this the report that gold was lavishly used in constructing Solomon's palace, and that ceremonial shields of solid gold lined the corridors of the greatest room (see 2 Chr. 9:15-20), and we can see why ton upon ton of gold would have been required to do what the Bible describes. It may not be too surprising to discover that a secular scholar once found the whole thing incredible, and called the story the product of an "exuberant imagination"!

But archaeologists have put the Bible's account in a different historical perspective. They have discovered that the rulers of the great civilizations of the ancient Middle East characteristically collected and stockpiled gold. In fact, in some centuries economic crises were caused by rulers who took too much gold out of circulation and stored it in their capital cities. So the flow of gold to Israel at this particular time in history is not at all out of harmony with what happened in other ancient lands.

But there's even more to the story of King Solomon's gold.

After Solomon's death he was succeeded by his son Rehoboam. Rehoboam's first act was to ignore foolishly the advice of his father's counselors and alienate the ten northern tribes of the united Hebrew kingdom (1 Kin. 11). The ten tribes seceded, and established a northern Hebrew kingdom ruled by

a man named Jeroboam. This left Rehoboam with the two
southern tribes, and with the capital city, Jerusalem.

At first Rehoboam responded to the prophets God sent to
guide him, and remained faithful to the Lord. But within a few
short years Rehoboam "forsook the law of the Lord, and all
Israel along with him" (2 Chr. 12:1). And so, just five short
years after Solomon died, God permitted the Egyptians under
Pharaoh Shishak to invade Rehoboam's kingdom. Shishak
captured Jerusalem. And the Egyptians stripped the temple
and the palace of all that gold!

How right Solomon had been in his lament! "I must leave
it to the man who will come after me," Solomon had written,
"And who knows whether he will be wise or a fool" (Eccl. 2:18,
19). Solomon had left his greatest works to his son Rehoboam.
And Rehoboam had turned out to be a fool! The gold that
Solomon had collected, the gold he had used to beautify his
greatest building projects, was taken away.

But what happened to all that gold? Surprisingly, we
know. We know because the year after Shishak sacked
Jerusalem and took the gold, he died and was succeeded by
Osorkon I. And Osorkon erected a granite pillar at Bubastis,
expressing his gratitude to the gods, and recording a
magnificent gift he made to them. That granite pillar describes
how Osorkon distributed ton upon ton of silver and ton upon
ton of gold to various temples and shrines in Egypt.

And that was hardly fair! Again Solomon was wise, and
correct. His own "labor [was] with wisdom and knowledge and
skill, yet he must leave his heritage to a man who has not
labored for it." In this case it was even worse. Solomon had
labored to beautify God's temple—and the gold he gathered
ended up in pagan shrines.

So we do know what happened to Solomon's gold. It was
stripped from the temple of God in Jerusalem, taken as booty
to Egypt, and distributed to the shrines that held the idols
representing the pagan deities of that ancient land.

All of Solomon's wealth, all of his accomplishments, went
for nothing.

And so we see why Solomon, who used his wealth as
wisely as any man could, was right when he concluded that it

was all meaningless. Solomon had used wealth wisely. But Solomon found no satisfaction in what he had accomplished.

And, perhaps even worse, even though Solomon had used much of his wealth to honor God in the temple he constructed, even this came to nothing.

All a person can do is to do his best.

Actually, even if Solomon's son hadn't been foolish and exposed his kingdom to the raiding Egyptians, Solomon's gold would have been taken in time. During the 384-year existence of the Southern Kingdom, Jerusalem was captured by no less than five foreign enemies. If Shishak hadn't taken King Solomon's gold, another conqueror would have claimed it.

What then did Solomon conclude? All a person can do is to do his best, to eat and to drink and to enjoy as much as he can the brief moment of life each of us is given under the sun. But one thing no person can possibly do. No person can possibly find life's meaning in wealth, or in the things that money can buy. Even if we use great wealth as wisely as possible, wealth has no potential for giving life ultimate meaning.

FOR REFLECTION

1. What would you do if you won $24 million at Lotto?

_____

_____

_____

2. The author commends Solomon for his wise use of his vast wealth. Do you think Solomon used his wealth wisely? Why, or why not? What might he have done differently?

_____

_____

_____

3. Solomon seems to have concluded that it is a good thing to enjoy our work and to enjoy food and drink during our lifetime. But he is convinced that having and using wealth cannot provide life with meaning, or give us fulfillment. How does what happened to King Solomon's gold illustrate his reasons for this conviction?

_____

_____

_____

Before reading the next chapter, meditate on this article on Luke 2:22–24 from the Personal Growth™ Study Bible.

The Old Testament made sure that every Jew could approach God and worship. When the sacrifice of a lamb was required, God permitted the very poor to bring instead a pair of cheap birds (see Lev. 12:2, 8). So the sacrifice described here underlines the poverty of the home in which God chose to place His Son.

There would be no "advantages" for Jesus. None of the toys indulgent moms and dads today buy so casually. None of the "IN" clothes teens today feel are so essential. Jesus wouldn't be sent to the best schools. His life would be hard. Even as a child He would contribute by working alongside Joseph as a carpenter's helper. God didn't want "advantages" for His Son.

Instead God chose to place Jesus in a home where simple people loved and honored the Lord. A home where constant need made for constant dependence on God. A home where spiritual values far outweighed material possessions. And so we wonder. Who grew up with life's true advantages? The affluent young of today? Or Jesus?

ME FIRST

Solomon's sudden sense of futility despite all his accomplishments has shaken the king. He is overwhelmed by a sense of meaninglessness. But Solomon isn't prepared to give up. He has too strong a sense of personal identity. Solomon exists. He simply can't accept the idea that his existence has no meaning at all.

It doesn't take a philosopher to have a sense of personal importance. We all have that sense. The infant who waves its arms and screams when hungry is letting the world know it is important. The newborn lacks words to express his or her sense of self, but every action shouts "ME first!"

We moms and dads see it as our children grow. They want this or that toy. They resent bedtime. They want the channel tuned to their TV show. As they reach adolescence, they demand the kind of clothes that their friends wear, grumble about schoolwork, and can't wait to get their driver's license. They worry about their looks, stand in front of the mirror combing their hair endlessly, and are devastated at the report of what that special boy or girl is supposed to have said about them.

When they're finally ready to go off to college or to enter the workforce they shop carefully for their wardrobe, worry about finding new friends, and although insecure are eager to make their own right or wrong choices without worrying about pleasing Mom and Dad. They plunge into a round of pleasures or else work hard to prepare for the future success they dream that they will have.

And few of us, throughout the years of childhood, adolescence, young adulthood, and on to maturity, ever stop to consider whether or not "I" am important. We simply assume. Of course "I" am important!

Everything we do, every choice we make, every dream we dream, is rooted in the sense that "I" am supremely important. "ME first" isn't selfishness. "ME first" is simply a reflection of the fact that our perspective is necessarily shaped by the fact that we experience life as ourselves, not someone else. Who we are, how we feel, what we value, is naturally important—to us.

Given this reality "ME first," the assumption that "I" am truly significant in the whole scheme of things, is completely understandable.

But what happens when we carefully examine our assumption of personal significance?

Solomon's Meditations

In his search for evidence of his own and every other individual's significance Solomon probed several avenues. He looked for personal significance in the patterns established in nature. He looked for personal significance in the fact of God's existence. He looked for personal significance in the destiny of all living creatures. And he looked for personal significance in the relationships we establish with one another. Yet after careful consideration Solomon was forced to the conclusion he had reached earlier.

W̶ho we are,
how we feel,
what we value,
is naturally
important—
to us.

Life is meaningless.

Everything is meaningless.

Even "I" am insignificant, despite the fact that we look at and experience life from our own self-centered points of view.

But how did Solomon reach these conclusions?

There is no evidence of personal significance in the patterns found in nature. One of the best-known passages in the Bible is Ecclesiastes 3. It's especially well-known in our time as lyrics put to music by the Byrds, often played on oldies stations. Solomon looks at nature and observes that for everything there is a season, a time for every purpose under heaven.

A time to be born,
  And a time to die;
A time to plant,
  And a time to pluck what is planted;
A time to kill,
  And a time to heal;

A time to break down,
　And a time to build up;
A time to weep,
　And a time to laugh;
A time to mourn,
　And a time to dance;
A time to cast away stones,
　And a time to gather stones;
A time to embrace,
　And a time to refrain from embracing;
A time to gain,
　And a time to lose;
A time to keep,
　And a time to throw away;
A time to tear,
　And a time to sew;
A time to keep silence,
　And a time to speak;
A time to love,
　And a time to hate;
A time of war,
　And a time of peace.

Ecclesiastes 3:2–8

For most of us the rhythms of this classic poem seem restful. We are comfortable with it, it seems right and natural. The repeated patterns, the cycles of life and death, of planting and reaping, the repetition of the seasons, provide us with a sense of stability. We feel comfortable, for we feel that whatever comes, these patterns provide a framework within which humanity can be secure.

But Solomon is not interested in the patterns as evidence of nature's stability. Solomon probes the patterns for evidence of his personal significance. And no evidence of personal significance can be found! Whether he lives or dies these cycles roll on, repeating themselves endlessly. They have existed from the dawn of history, and as far as Solomon can tell will continue endlessly.

Whether Solomon lives or dies.

Whether any individual lives or dies.

In the patterns established in nature Solomon can only find evidence that the individual is *insignificant*. Whatever a person may accomplish in his or her brief years on Earth will have no impact at all on the impersonal cycles of nature that link past and present and future without regard to any person, however much each individual might yearn to feel that "I" count.

There is no evidence of personal significance in the fact that God exists. Unlike moderns who have invented evolution in a frantic effort to make God irrelevant, Solomon is convinced that God exists. This is plain to Solomon from two clear lines of evidence. First, "He has made everything beautiful" (3:11).

Philosophers call this the "argument from design." Creation has an order and pattern, a complexity and functionality that can be rationally explained only by the existence of a Designer. Solomon, a close student of nature and cataloger of plants and animals, has observed this order and been awed by the beauty of God's grand design.

God simply does not *need* us. God is complete in Himself.

Second, Solomon recognizes another compelling reason to believe that God exists. God, Solomon says, "has put eternity in their hearts" (3:11). Human beings intuitively realize that there is more to reality than this world of time and space. What's more, human beings have an inexplicable conviction that biological death cannot be the end.

But Solomon's conviction that God exists fails to solve his problem. How does the existence of God make the individual significant? In fact, the very otherness of a God great enough to create makes humans seem *insignificant*. Solomon writes,

> I know that whatever God does,
> It shall be forever.
> Nothing can be added to it,
> And nothing taken from it.
> *Ecclesiastes 3:14*

God simply does not *need* us. God is complete in Himself. He plans and carries out His works without seeking our help. There is nothing we can add to what God has done, and nothing we can do to take away from it. We are subject to God's judgment (3:17), and this has an impact on *us*. But whether we are righteous or wicked has no impact on *Him*.

In terms of a human's influence on God, as in terms of a human's impact on the cycles of nature, the individual has no significance at all. Our life, Solomon argues, is meaningless.

There is no evidence of personal significance in the destiny of living creatures. Because God has planted eternity in our hearts, humankind has an intuitive belief that death cannot end an individual's existence. But Solomon has determined to use his reason and carefully examine only the evidence available to him in this world. From all Solomon can observe, human beings are "like animals."

In a much misunderstood meditation, Solomon sums up his conclusion.

> For what happens to the sons of men also happens to animals; one thing befalls them: as one dies, so dies the other. Surely, they all have one breath; man has no advantage over animals, for all is vanity.
>
> All go to one place: all are from the dust, and all return to dust. Who knows the spirit of the sons of men, which goes upward, and the spirit of the animal, which goes down to the earth?
>
> *Ecclesiastes 3:19–21*

Solomon's point is that, from what he can observe in nature, the death of a man is no different from the death of an animal. His last observation is better translated, "who knows *if* the spirit of a man goes upward, while the spirit of an animal goes downward into the earth?" From what a person limited to this world can see, there is no evidence of a "human spirit" which survives the death of the body.

This conclusion is hardly unique to Solomon. The Roman poet Lucretius in "The Arms of Nemesis," published around 55 B.C., has these thoughts on death.

> What has death to frighten man,
> If souls can die as bodies can?

When mortal frame shall be disbanded,
This lump of flesh from life unhanded,
From grief and pain we shall be free—
We shall not *feel*, for we shall not *be*.
But suppose that after meeting Fate
The soul still feels in its divided state.
What's that to us? For we are only *we*
While body and soul in one frame agree.
And if our atoms should revolve by chance
And our cast-off matter rejoin the dance,
What gain to us would all this bring?
This new-made man would be a new-made thing.
We, dead and gone, would play no part
In all the pleasures, nor feel the smart
Which to that new man shall accrue
Whom of our matter Time molds anew.
Take heart then, listen and hear;
What is there left in death to fear?
After the pause of life has come between,
All's just the same had we never been.

Sorry sentiments indeed for anyone as desperate as Solomon to find some evidence in life or death of personal significance. "All's just the same had we never been."

"Meaningless," Solomon concludes.

Life is meaningless, and the notion of personal fulfillment is nothing but an empty dream.

There is no evidence of personal significance in the relationships we establish with others. Solomon has searched nature, pondered the existence of God, and meditated on death in his search for personal significance. He also has carefully observed human behavior.

What set Solomon on one possibly fruitful line of thought was observing a person who had no living relatives. The man was active, enthusiastic, and eager in the pursuit of riches. He drove himself to pile up treasures without thought of rest or pleasure. And Solomon shook his head in wonder, for "he never asks, 'For whom do I toil and deprive myself of good'" (4:8).

The image of this isolated, lonely man stood as a symbol to Solomon of meaninglessness and "grave misfortune." But it also set him thinking. Perhaps there is meaning to be found in our relationships. Solomon quickly saw the advantages of establishing personal bonds with others.

> Two are better than one,
> Because they have a good reward for their labor.
> For if they fall, one will lift up his companion.
> But woe to him who is alone when he falls,
> For he has no one to help him up.
> Again, if two lie down together, they will keep warm;
> But how can one be warm alone?
> Though one may be overpowered by another, two
>   can withstand him.
> And a threefold cord is not quickly broken.
>
> *Ecclesiastes 4:9–12*

But these advantages to the individual of a close relationship with some other hardly helps Solomon establish his personal significance. After all, the individuals we accept as our partners in life are just as insignificant, in any ultimate sense, as we are. A partner's life or death leaves nature's patterns unaffected. A partner's life or death does not and cannot change God. And when a partner dies, there is no evidence to be found in this world that he or she still exists as a conscious, personal being.

And we, once again, are left alone.

FOR REFLECTION

1. Solomon seems to feel that if life is to have meaning, he as an individual must be significant. Do you agree or disagree? _____

2. Most of us simply assume that we are significant as individuals. This is in part because, the author suggests, we see life from our own personal perspective. How would you go about demonstrating that you truly are significant?

_____

_____

_____

3. Solomon's research led him to the conclusion that life is meaningless because his reasoning led him to conclude that the individual simply is not significant. Can you sum up each of his arguments? Which seems most compelling to you?

_____

_____

_____

Before reading the next chapter, meditate on this article on Genesis 2:2, from the Personal Growth™ *Study Bible.*

There are times we don't feel special. Parents may have criticized us so harshly that we grew up feeling worthless. We may look at successful friends and feel like failures. It's then we need to let God remind us that we bear His image and likeness.

Genesis 1 says God created galaxies of stars simply by speaking a word. But in Genesis 2:7 we see God stoop down to personally shape the human form, and breathe into us His breath of life. By this act we were given the unique gifts of being able to think and feel and choose—abilities possessed only by God.

Next time you're down on yourself, sense God bending down to breathe fresh life into you. You share God's image and His likeness. You truly are special. And you are special to Him.

TOP OF THE HEAP

I don't know whether or not you've ever played the game, but it's a fun one. It's called, "If I were in charge. . . ."

All you need to do to play the game is make a list of ten things you would do if you were in charge of the country. Get some friends to make their lists, and then compare.

There are some rules, of course. You can't list results. For instance, you can't say, "I'd end drug traffic." Now, you can say, "I'd pass a law that anyone selling drugs will be executed." That's something you could do if you were really in charge, and that might very well stop drug traffic. But when you're playing "If I were in charge, . . ." you have to state means without identifying ends.

Now, if I were in charge, here are a few of the things I would consider doing:

1. I'd require high school graduation to get a driver's license.
2. I'd give parents vouchers and permit them to choose public or private grade and high schools for their children.
3. I'd require a balanced federal budget now, not in seven or in ten years.
4. I'd end welfare as such, but supplement the pay of an ex-welfare recipient through the employer who provides an entry-level job with advancement potential, to provide a living wage.
5. I'd end all farm subsidies, and especially those on tobacco.
6. I'd impose jail sentences only on those found guilty of violent crimes. Others would be supervised and sentenced to make restitution to those they harmed.
7. I'd establish a flat income tax on all income from any source, with NO loopholes.
8. I'd require rigorous testing for anyone seeking to gain entrance to a four-year college.

9. I'd require both plaintiffs and lawyers to pay the costs of civil suits which they lose: the plaintiff to pay the defendant, and the lawyers to pay the opposing side's costs and attorney fees.

10. I'd establish two-term limits for Congress members and for senators, as well as for the president.

Now, you may or may not like what I'd do if I were in charge. Personally, I think taking these steps would make things better in our country, for all of its citizens. But there's a more important question to ask if we're following Solomon's train of thought, and engaged with him in his inquiry:

Would being in charge make *me* significant? Would I be fulfilled if I were in control?

Solomon's answer to this question is obvious. Solomon *was* in charge. Solomon was an autocratic ruler in an age where the word of kings was law. Solomon could and did order the execution of those he determined were criminals. He was judge and jury. Solomon could and did order the aliens in Israel to go to work on his temple project. Solomon could and did reorganize the government, promote and demote officials, and raise taxes *as he chose*.

This certainly made Solomon the most important person in his kingdom. Compared to others, he was more significant by far. But was this enough? Did this give Solomon a sense of fulfillment? Did the knowledge that he was in charge give him a sense of *ultimate* significance?

The answer, of course, is "No." Despite the fact that Solomon was in charge, despite the fact that he was the most significant person in all Israel, the king was driven to the conclusion that life is vanity. Everything is meaningless.

The fact that he was king was meaningless.

The fact that he *lived* was meaningless.

Now, it's true that if we change the rules of inquiry to consider what God has revealed to us in His Word our conclusion will be very different. But Solomon limited himself to consider only what he could see and experience. Based on the evidence of what he observed, and on his powers of reason, Solomon was forced to believe that his life—that human life itself—has no meaning at all.

The Limitations on Control

When people today think of personal fulfillment they tend to assume they may find it in one of three ways.

For some, fulfillment is sought in achievement. Even those who are forced to do menial work to support themselves still assume that, if they only had the time and the money, they could find fulfillment in what they could then achieve.

For others, fulfillment is sought in self-indulgence. They see themselves as the center of the universe. If life were arranged to meet all their needs, to satisfy all their wants, life would be fulfilling.

For still others fulfillment is sought in controlling others. If people would do things *their* way, if their opinion were what counted, if they were in charge, everything would be put right. And they, personally, would be fulfilled.

That's why Solomon's book of Ecclesiastes is so unsettling. Solomon had untold wealth and used it to accomplish great projects. But none of his achievements gave his life meaning, and he felt unfulfilled. Solomon was able to indulge his every desire, but when Solomon was challenged to ask if he, himself, were really significant, he was forced to conclude that he really was not. What fulfillment could there be in indulging his wants if he and his wants were totally irrelevant in the grand scheme of things? Solomon, as an autocratic ruler, was undoubtedly the most significant person in his kingdom. But as Solomon considered this fact, he realized that his ability to control others was unable to provide that sense of life's meaning for which he yearned. Why?

God is the One who is truly in charge, not Solomon. Solomon is significant when he compares himself to others. After all, as king he is in charge. But when Solomon compares himself with God, he realizes that he isn't in charge at all. Others may have to walk softly around him. But he must walk softly around God!

"Walk prudently when you go to the house of God,"

> When people today think of personal fulfillment, they tend to assume it is found in achievement, self-indulgence, or in controlling others.

Solomon advises. "Draw near to hear rather than to give the sacrifice of fools" (Eccl. 5:1). Solomon's choice of words is significant. In Hebrew the idiom "to hear" implies "to obey." Solomon approaches God not as one who is in control, but as one who is subject to a far higher Power. But what is the "sacrifice of fools"? It is the sacrifice that the Law requires a person offer when he or she has sinned unintentionally (see Lev. 1—5). The foolish person is morally deficient from a lack of knowledge of God's will; "they do not know that they do evil."

Solomon continues in this vein for several verses.

> Do not be rash with your mouth,
> And let not your heart utter anything
>   hastily before God.
> For God is in heaven, and you on earth;
> Therefore let your words be few.
>
> *Ecclesiastes 5:2*

> When you make a vow to God, do not
>   delay to pay it;
> For He has not pleasure in fools.
> Pay what you have vowed—
> Better not to vow than to vow and not pay.
>
> *Ecclesiastes 5:4*

> Do not let your mouth cause your flesh
> to sin, nor say before the messenger
> of God that it was an error. Why should
> God be angry at your excuse and destroy
> the work of your hands?
>
> *Ecclesiastes 5:6*

Solomon may exercise control over those in his kingdom. But Solomon himself is severely limited by his awareness of God's ultimate control over the universe and over human affairs.

Some with power may swell with pride and look around arrogantly, as if they were the measure of all things. Solomon is too wise to fall into this trap. He realizes completely that with all his power he himself is powerless before God.

Being in charge, in control of the lives of so many others, has not fulfilled Solomon or made him truly significant.

Solomon's power over others is apparent rather than real. To anyone observing Solomon it might appear that his power over others is unlimited. But this notion that one person can truly exercise authority over other people is a fiction rather than a reality.

Solomon is a good ruler whose intent is to judge the nation wisely and root out injustice. Yet anyone traveling through his kingdom will find incidents of injustice abound. How can this be? Solomon says,

> If you see the oppression of the poor, and the violent perversion of justice and righteousness in a province, do not marvel at the matter; for high official watches over high official, and higher officials are over them.
>
> *Ecclesiastes 5:8*

What Solomon is saying is that he may give commands, but he must rely on a bureaucracy to carry out his commands. How do we explain corruption in a land ruled by a godly king? Why, the king's orders must pass through layer after layer of officials, each of whom has his own mind, and each of whom may reinterpret what the king has said to his own advantage.

This is an important concept. Is it really possible to control others? We may have power. We may give commands. But there is no way that we can guarantee that what we decide will actually be done. Even a parent, who controls a child's bedtime, can't force the child to go to sleep. We may say, "Go to bed," and force the child to do so. But there is no way we can force that child to close his or her eyes and sleep.

The idea that we can control any other person is fiction.

Ultimately the idea that we can control any other person is fiction, no more than a pretense that may fool the arrogant, but cannot stand up to the scrutiny of a wise person who looks at life as it really is.

Solomon's power over possessions is also apparent rather than real. During Solomon's reign wealth poured into Israel.

Solomon became unimaginably wealthy. And many others in that blessed land became rich too. Certainly being in charge enables a person to assemble great wealth.

Earlier Solomon looked at wealth as a means which enabled him to undertake and achieve great things. In despair he concluded that his achievements were worthless. Now Solomon looks at power over others as a means to assemble wealth for its own sake. The trouble is, wealth gathered for its own sake is also meaningless. Wealth in itself can never satisfy.

> He who loves silver will not be satisfied with silver;
> Nor he who loves abundance, with increase.
> This also is vanity.
>
> *Ecclesiastes 5:10*

Not only does wealth fail to satisfy the empty heart, the possession of wealth increases expenses. The more one has, the more he or she spends.

> When goods increase,
> They increase who eat them;
> So what profit have the owners
> Except to see them with their eyes.
>
> *Ecclesiastes 5:11*

In fact, using one's power to gather wealth makes life more trying rather than easier. The person who works hard for his or her food and shelter can sleep peacefully. "But the abundance of the rich will not permit him to sleep" (5:12). The rich worry about their wealth, and fear its loss. The man or woman with little is freed from such concerns.

Even if the person in power keeps the wealth safe throughout his or her lifetime, it means nothing to him or her in the end.

> As he came from his mother's womb,
>   naked shall he return,
> To go as he came.
> And he shall take nothing from his labor
> Which he may carry away in his hand.

And this also is a severe evil—
Just exactly as he came, so shall he go.
And what profit has he who has labored for the wind?
All his days he also eats in darkness,
And he has much sorrow and sickness and anger.

Ecclesiastes 5:15–17

And so Solomon comes to the end of his quest here at the conclusion of Chapter five. In the rest of the book Solomon asks a different question. There he asks whether some ways are better than others in view of the fact that life is essentially meaningless. And, wise man that he is, Solomon concludes that yes, some conditions are to be preferred.

But always, ever, Solomon's conviction remains the same. No one who seeks to live life on his or her own, without God, and without divine guidance, will find meaning or fulfillment. Surely there is no fulfillment to be found in any great achievement. There is no meaning to be found in putting ME first, and satisfying every passing need or desire. There is no meaning to be found in our attempts to exercise control over others, whether to move them to do good, or to move them to provide us with great wealth.

For a person on his or her own, life is one thing and one thing only. Meaningless.

FOR REFLECTION

1. If you were in charge, what ten things would you do? Jot them down, and see how they compare with the ten listed by the author, or by other friends.

_____

_____

_____

2. Who in your family or on your job frustrates you most? What would you do if you were in full control of their lives for just one week?

_____

_____

_____

3. Solomon sees several limits on the power he has as king to truly control others or even to control his great wealth. Can you think of any reasons why it might be *harmful* to have control over others?

_____

_____

_____

Before reading the next chapter, meditate on these thoughts on Proverb 26:13–16 from the Personal Growth™ Study Bible.

There was a contest to determine the laziest man in the land. The first candidate was situationally lazy. He was only lazy when it came to things he didn't want to do. He kept making excuses not to go to work. "There's a lion in the streets" was his most creative excuse.

The second candidate was congenitally lazy. He didn't even bother to enter the contest. He simply rolled over in bed and went back to sleep.

The third candidate won. He was so lazy that though his hand was in the meal's main dish, he couldn't be bothered to lift it to his mouth to eat. He was fatally lazy.

Actually, all three candidates lost. They saw life as too meaningless to make an effort. But the Christian's life isn't meaningless. God calls on us to be steadfast, "always abounding in the work of the Lord," And He promises, "your labor is not in vain in the Lord" (1 Cor. 15:58).

ETERNITY IN THE HEART

*O*ur new puppy, a little less than a year old, is named Micah. He's a wiggly, happy dog, who bounds out awkwardly and eagerly to meet anyone who comes to our door. We found him at the local flea market, walked by him at first, and then as we were driving out of the parking lot realized we just couldn't leave him behind. Micah was welcomed by our five-year-old dog, Mitzi, and the two now play endlessly, chasing each other until both lie panting, exhausted on the floor.

Micah's also been a delight to my wife, an affectionate friend who rushes to leap up beside her when she sits down and tries to cover her with wet doggy kisses. Despite the fact that Micah has chewed a hole in one chair, gnawed on the leg of what was Sue's grandmother's table, and ruined some six pairs of shoes, our little dog remains welcome. Of course, whenever we go out now we lock him in a bathroom where he can do minimum damage. But Micah doesn't seem to hold it against us. When we return he leaps in excitement, races around the house, and isn't satisfied until he's barreled into every family member to show his delight at our return. Who could help loving little Micah, despite his destructive tendencies? Certainly we can't.

Yet we never stop to wonder if life seems meaningless to Micah. We never wonder if Micah will find fulfillment. To even raise such questions makes no sense at all. Micah is a dog. He has a personality that is all his own, yet he lives in the moment and responds as instinct directs. God has not seen fit to do for dogs what He has done for us human beings. In Solomon's words, God has "put eternity in our hearts."

Micah can find his destiny within the confines of his life in time and space, and never give a thought to what lies beyond. But you and I have a destiny that stretches far beyond time. While we live today in our own here and now, the fact that God has put eternity in our hearts links our destiny to

Him. Biological death is not the end for you or me. It is the passage to another phase of existence, in a "forever" that will never end.

It is this, our link with eternity, that leads human beings to question life's meaning and to yearn for fulfillment. It is our link with God and eternity, whether a given individual is aware of that link or not, that leads human beings to feel that simply living is not enough. We must have something to live *for*.

Micah never raises questions like these. Micah never has that uncomfortable feeling that there must be more to life than he experiences. God has not put eternity in Micah's heart.

God has put eternity in ours.

Created in God's Image

In creating humankind in His image, God provided us with unique gifts and potentials. In creating us in His image God gave us a capacity of mind and imagination that makes achievement possible, and which drives us to create and to do. In creating us in His image God gave us self-awareness, with an innate sense of our personal significance. In creating us in His image God gave us a moral awareness, which leads us to identify certain things as right and others as wrong. With that gift has come the conviction that our standards are right, and should be adopted by others.

The drive to achieve, the sense of self-importance, the moral convictions that lead us to believe that we know best, are all gifts from God. The problem we have is that through sin we are linked with eternity, and although it is very real, it has become insubstantial to us. Sin has corrupted our race, and one of its consequences is that we human beings *misunderstand the use of* God's gifts. We live our lives isolated from God, and try to find meaning not by relating our capacities to

> **I**t is our link with God and eternity that leads human beings to feel that simply living is not enough. We must have something to live *for*.

eternity, but by focusing our exercise of our gifts on projects in this present world.

As we've seen, that was Solomon's approach when he set out to find life's meaning. Solomon accomplished great things in his world and time. But that time is long gone, and nothing Solomon accomplished remains. Solomon spared no effort to satisfy his every need and desire. But Solomon's body long ago faded into dust, and what he felt then as needs to be satisfied are irrelevant today. Solomon exercised control over others through his wealth and through the power he possessed as an absolute ruler. But Solomon's kingdom, and the men and women he ruled, passed long ago off this world's stage.

Simply put, we who have eternity in our hearts should not expect to find fulfillment in anything we achieve, in any needs that are met, or in any authority over others that is exercised during our brief years of existence in the material universe. God shared His image and likeness with us, and gave us our wonderful gifts and abilities, that we might use them to impact eternity and not simply time.

> God shared His image and likeness with us, and gave us our wonderful gifts and abilities, that we might use them to impact eternity and not simply time.

It's quite natural, of course, that we human beings, cut off as we are from God by sin, should expect to find life's meaning in this life. It's natural to expect to find fulfillment by using God's gifts to us in the here and now.

Even Christians are likely to operate on assumptions that drive the unsaved. We too feel the need to achieve in this world. We too strongly feel that our present needs should be met. And we too feel that others in our homes and churches should do what we believe is best and right. The very existence of these marvelous gifts that God has given us convinces us that somehow we have a right to achieve, a right to have our needs met, and a right to influence or even control others. And much of what we do is guided by our assumptions about *how* to achieve, *how* to have our needs met, and *how* to influence others.

The trouble is, when we human beings are left on our own, *we don't really* know how to use our gifts to find the fulfillment we yearn for.

Nathaniel, whom we met in the first chapter, was delighted to at last have a plot of land of his own. It was something he had worked for and dreamed of having. It was important to him; it was a foundation on which he could build for his family. When a neighbor seemed intent on defrauding him of some of that land, Nathaniel was upset. Any of us would have been. Then, as it became clear that the dispute could not be resolved, Nathaniel became more and more angry. He even misused his pulpit to attack his neighbor.

It wasn't just the land, although being able to purchase it was a significant achievement for Nathaniel. It was the fact that the land was rightly *his*, and the neighbor who was trying to take it from him was in the wrong.

In a situation like this most of us would insist on our rights. We would fight for the land that was rightly ours. We would want to *win*. So we can understand why Nathaniel used every means at his disposal, every ability which God had given him, to do just this. To win!

But then Nathaniel heard a Voice from outside of time. And that Voice redirected Nathaniel's attitude and changed his relationship with his neighbor.

Karen felt a nagging dissatisfaction with the people in her Bible study group. No one seemed to really care about *her*. She had needs that weren't being met; concerns that were not being addressed. She began to resent the others for their insensitivity, and for their selfish focus on their own concerns while totally ignoring hers.

Like the rest of us Karen felt that she was important; that she had a right to have her needs met. She didn't expect others to focus on her needs all the time. But was it too much to expect others to pay her just a little more attention?

Karen isn't a pushy person. She didn't go into the group and demand attention, although that seemed one possible solution. Instead she felt her resentment grow, and in retaliation Karen held back more and more. She looked at the others in her small Bible study group and noted their flaws, and even began to feel disdain for the petty issues that seemed to occupy their thoughts.

And then Karen heard a Voice speaking from outside of time. And that Voice redirected Karen's attitude and transformed her relationship with the others in her Bible study.

Liz couldn't help feeling judgmental about her family. They had been shocked and hurt when she found Christ outside their church. They had persecuted her, and hurt her deeply by their attitude. And all the time they were in the grip of doctrines that she *knew* were wrong.

As the years passed Liz became more and more convinced that her family simply had to see faith her way. She loved her family—her dad and mom, all the brothers and sisters, the nieces and nephews—but she simply *had* to convince them that she was right. When they failed to respond, when they refused to let go of their loyalty to the church in which they'd been brought up, the conflict in Liz became more and more terrible. She was loving but judgmental. She was deeply committed to her family, but at the same time they were no longer acceptable to her. They simply *had to change*. Liz had to do her best to *make* them change.

We focus the use of our God-given gifts on time rather than on eternity.

And then Liz too heard a Voice from outside of time. And that Voice redirected Liz's attitude and transformed her relationship with her family.

Life with God

It is our human nature itself, as God Himself designed it, that makes certain things important to us. Because we're made in God's image, we have a drive to achieve. Because we're made in God's image, we have a sense of our own personal importance. Because we're made in God's image we have a sense of what is right and what is wrong. It's only natural that we should expect to find fulfillment in exercising these gifts God has given us.

What Solomon did, however, was what most of us human beings do. *We focus the use of our God-given gifts on time rather than on eternity.* We too may undertake great building projects, or spend our lives building a fortune, and expect such achievements to give life meaning. But they will not. We too may seek relationships which we think will meet our needs, whether for pleasure or support, and hope that if others give us what we want we'll feel fulfilled. But we will not. We can try to manipulate others to accept our values and live by our convictions, and assume that by controlling others life will have more meaning for us. But it will not.

What Solomon needed, what we need, and what Nathaniel and Karen and Liz all heard, was a Voice from outside of time. We need to hear and respond to the Voice of God, telling each one of us *how* to live in time with eternity's values in view.

As God intended for us all along.

God's Gift of His Wisdom

Solomon was the wisest of men, and he used his wisdom to see whether human beings could find meaning in this life apart from God. He concluded that life on our own was essentially meaningless.

In 1 Corinthians 2 Paul wrote about our need for the "wisdom of God." His point is that human wisdom is flawed, for it is limited to what we can discover by observation and experience in this world. No human being can stand outside of time, in eternity, and see things from God's perspective. In making his point Paul quotes in verse 9 from the pagan poet Empedocles, who ridiculed the notion that human beings could ever know the meaning of life. That poet wrote,

Weak and narrow are the powers implanted in the limbs of man; many are the woes that fall on them and blunt the edges of thought; short is the measure of the life in death through which they toil. Then are they borne away; like smoke that vanished into the air; and what they dream they know is but the little that each hath stumbled upon in wandering about the world. Yet boast they all that they have learned the whole.

Vain fools! For what that is, no eye hath seen, no ear hath heard, nor can it be conceived by the mind of man.

But God knows the whole! God knows the true meaning of human life. And God knows how we can use the gifts He has given us to find fulfillment!

Paul goes on to remind us that "God has revealed them to us through His Spirit. . . . Now we have received, not the spirit of the world, but the Spirit who is from God, that we might know the things that have been freely given to us by God" (1 Cor. 2:11, 12).

God not only knows the meaning of life, God has revealed how we can use His gifts rightly, and so be fulfilled. Nathaniel heard God's Voice, and God's Word transformed his attitude toward his land and his relationship with his neighbor. Karen heard His Voice, and God's Word showed her how to find joy in meeting the needs of others. Liz heard His Voice, and God's Word brought her peace as it taught her to love her family unconditionally.

It is God's Word, a word from outside of time, that can teach us to use our gifts to build for eternity rather than time—and so be fulfilled.

FOR REFLECTION

1. The author makes much of the fact that human beings are created in the image of God. Why does he believe this is so important?

---

2. The gifts God has given us can be used to reach goals we might set for life in this world. But this use of our gifts cannot bring fulfillment. Why?

---

3. How did God's Voice, coming from outside of time through His Word, transform the ways that Nathaniel, Karen, and Liz used their God-given gifts? In what ways was following God's Word more fulfilling for each of them?

_____

_____

_____

Before reading the next chapter, meditate on this article on Psalm 119:105, from the Personal Growth™ Study Bible.

"Lord, do you want me to be a missionary when I finish college? I really want to know your will." We all want to know God's will. But prayers like this are seldom answered. Why? Psalm 119:105 suggests a reason. The verse describes God's Word as a "lamp to my feet, and a light to my path."

In biblical times persons who traveled at night carried an oil lamp or sheltered candle. These shed a circle of light just wide enough for an individual to take his next step safely. The light that God provides is no headlight, enabling us to see years ahead down our life's highway. God gives us just enough light to see our next step. As we take that step in His will, He provides enough light for the next step, and then for the next.

If we truly want to know God's will we need to pray, "Lord, show me what you want me to do today." Live each day in the center of God's will, and we can leave the years ahead in His hand.

BUILDING BIG
AND BEAUTIFUL

When we read the description of Solomon's temple in Jerusalem, we're impressed. Every detail is so carefully planned. Of course, we can't give all the credit to Solomon, although he supervised the actual construction. First Chronicles 28:11, 12 tells us that David designed the temple, and gave Solomon "the plans for all that he [David] had [received] by the Spirit." The temple was simply too important for its details to be left to even as brilliant a man as Solomon.

Actually, it is the other architectural works of Solomon that impress us with his skill as a builder. Nothing remains of his palace. But archaeologists have been able to reconstruct features of some of the cities that Solomon fortified. In the ancient world the most vulnerable part of any fortified city's walls were the gates. When Solomon strengthened the fortifications of Megeddo, a city located in the Valley of Jezreel on the trade route between Syria and Egypt, he designed a complex gate system. There were the traditional two strong towers above the gate, and the extended entry passage through which any enemy must pass to enter the city. But there was also a complex of towers, stairs, and steep roadway that extended out in front of the gate, and multiplied difficulties for any attacking army. Some archaeologists see this gate system, found in other Israelite cities of the same era, as one of Solomon's most significant innovations.

Solomon had skills as a builder in different arenas as well. He built a relationship with Hiram of Tyre, a traditional sea power, which enabled Solomon alone of all Israel's kings to build a trading fleet. During Solomon's reign this fleet brought billions of dollars worth of trade goods into Israel by sea, a much cheaper way of transporting goods than by caravans traveling the long-established overland trade routes. In effect Solomon built the equivalent of a Fortune 500 company.

There are other arenas too in which Solomon proved himself a wise builder. Solomon was a far-sighted nation-builder. Throughout the years from the conquest to the monarchy, tribal boundaries had been maintained, and individuals identified themselves by their tribe. We can understand this, as before the Civil War many thought of themselves as Mississippians or New Yorkers rather than simply as Americans. In fact, when the southern states first seceded, Robert E. Lee was offered command of the Union armies—but decided reluctantly that his allegiance was to his home state of Virginia. Solomon sensed the danger of tribal allegiance, and one of his innovations was to establish administrative districts which cut across the old tribal lines (1 Kin. 4:1–19). Solomon's intent was to strengthen the central government, and gradually weaken the tribal system so that individuals would in time identify themselves first of all as Israelites. The need for such nation-building is illustrated by the fact that after Solomon's death the ten northern tribes seceded from the south, and the national unity Solomon sought to carefully build was shattered.

In fact, if we look back at all of Solomon's accomplishments, we realize that despite his genius, nothing that he achieved has survived. The national unity he worked to create was shattered immediately after his death. The trading fleets he organized were disbanded, and no other Jewish king was ever able to establish a Hebrew presence on the seas. And every city that Solomon fortified fell to Israel's enemies. Solomon used the great gifts God had given him to build material things. But, as Solomon himself realized as he neared the end of his life, it was all meaningless.

Nothing survived.

Even the temple on which Solomon lavished so much attention was burned to ashes by the Babylonians and its remaining treasures taken to that foreign land.

Building for Eternity

It's helpful for us to compare Solomon with Nathaniel. Like Solomon, this young African is a gifted individual, intent on achievement. He left his homeland to study at Philadelphia College of Bible, where he earned his way working on the campus. When Nathaniel returned to Africa it was to pastor his home church.

Nathaniel has a family, and like any father he wants to do his best for them. When the opportunity came to buy land on which Nathaniel could grow food and other crops, he was thrilled. Land was and is a foundation on which to build a more secure future for the family. So Nathaniel, like Solomon, was using his God-given gifts to build for the future. He sacrificed to receive the training that equipped him for ministry. And he seized the opportunity to become a landowner.

And then one neighbor stubbornly refused to allow him clear title to the land he had purchased. Despite proof after proof that Nathaniel was in the right, the neighbor insisted that a disputed half-acre belonged to him.

Nathaniel has told us how in his frustration he became more and more angry. Nathaniel has told us how he misused his pulpit to preach pointed sermons on honesty and justice that were in fact thinly disguised attacks on his neighbor.

And Nathaniel has told us how God spoke to him through a passage in Jesus' Sermon on the Mount. That Voice, from outside of time, convicted Nathaniel and told him what he must do. Nathaniel, the person who was wronged, must go and be reconciled to his neighbor. Truly repentant, Nathaniel did go to his neighbor, "immediately." Nathaniel confessed his sinful attitude and asked forgiveness. Nathaniel writes, "when he saw what I did, he asked forgiveness also. We forgave each other."

A few days later the neighbor offered a solution to the dispute over the field and, again in Nathaniel's words, "our relationship was repaired, our fellowship grew, and our worship of God became whole."

What had emerged from this experience was a unique building of the inner lives of Nathaniel, his family, his neighbor, and ultimately the inner lives of the members of his church as well.

The Ability to Build

When God made us in His own image, He gave us marvelous capacities to build and construct. Many use these God-given gifts to build buildings or fortunes or reputations in this world. Christians are to use these God-given gifts to build their own and others' inner lives.

In Ephesians 4 the apostle Paul writes about gifted individuals that Christ has given the Church, not to build themselves, but to equip believers for their work of building.

> He Himself [Christ] gave some to be apostles, some prophets, some evangelists, and some pastors and teachers, for the equipping of the saints for the work of ministry, for the edifying of the body of Christ, till we all come to the unity of the faith and of the knowledge of the Son of God, to a perfect man, to the measure of the stature of the fullness of Christ.
>
> *Ephesians 4:11–13*

A key word here is "edifying," which is a translation of the Greek word *oikodome*. Both this Greek noun and the Greek verb are often used in the New Testament with the meaning of "building up," or "strengthening." In fact, the noun is used in this sense in 1 Corinthians 8:1; 10:23; 14:4, 17; and 1 Thessalonians 5:11, while the verb is used in this sense in Romans 14:19, 15:2; 1 Corinthians 14:2, 5, 12, 26; 2 Corinthians 10:8, 12:19, 13:10; and Ephesians 4:12, 16, and 29. As we can see, the building metaphor is an important one in the New Testament. And what we build is one another's inner lives!

Christians are to use God-given gifts to build their own and others' inner lives.

Holy Temples

Solomon constructed a temple of quarried stone which he covered with gold inside and outside. In his first letter Peter presents a striking contrast. "You also, as living stones, are being built up a spiritual house" (1 Pet. 2:5). What God is concerned with building today is the believer.

The apostle Paul uses the same image in 1 Corinthians 6:19, 20. "Or do you not know that your body is the temple of the Holy Spirit who is in you, whom you have from God, and you are not your own? For you were bought at a price; therefore glorify God in your body and in your spirit, which are God's." Today we are God's temple. God's work is one of redesigning you and me, of constructing within us a character which will bring Him glory.

Note the contrasts between the temple Solomon built and the temple God is building today.

Solomon used people to build God a temple.
God is rebuilding our inner lives that we might be a fit temple, housing His presence.

Solomon's temple was constructed from quarried stones.
God's temple today is being constructed of living stones.

Solomon's temple was material.
God's temple today is spiritual.

God came to dwell in Solomon's temple.
God's Spirit dwells today in our lives.

Solomon's temple was set apart to God.
Today we are to be set apart, called to glorify God in our daily lives.

Solomon's temple fell into ruin and ultimately was destroyed.
God's temple today cannot be destroyed, for with eternity in our hearts, we are destined to live with Him forever and ever.

Solomon, who looked for fulfillment in using his God-given abilities to build structures of stone, felt that life was meaningless. Today you and I can find meaning and fulfillment by using our God-given abilities to build grace into the inner lives of others who love Jesus as we do.

This is the real significance of Nathaniel's experience. As long as the land had primary importance for Nathaniel, and his focus was on what he was trying to achieve in this world, he was frustrated, angry, and miserable. He even used his pulpit and the Bible to break down his neighbor's resistance, and shame the neighbor into surrendering his claim to the land Nathaniel was sure that he owned. But then God spoke to Nathaniel's heart.

God refocused Nathaniel's priorities. As God ministered in Nathaniel's heart, reconciliation with his neighbor became more important than any worldly achievement or possession. God then used Nathaniel's apology to soften his neighbor's heart, and to reconcile the two as brothers. Yes, out of this reconciliation a solution to the land problem emerged. But what was truly important was that when Nathaniel reordered his priorities, he became more worthy and beautiful as a dwelling place for God. And that through Nathaniel's willingness to confess and seek reconciliation, his neighbor too became a more worthy and beautiful dwelling for the Lord.

> **D**iscover the joy of building lives, not fortunes or reputations.

Nathaniel had discovered the joy of using his gifts to build lives, not fortunes or reputations. Nathaniel had discovered that the use of his abilities to build lives could and did bring fulfillment.

Perhaps the most important concern that emerges from the use of the building metaphor in the New Testament is: How do we build? What can we do that contributes to the inner lives of others? In a later chapter we'll look more carefully at guidelines for God's builders. But we can get a pretty good idea of how we can build by simply surveying those passages where the noun or verb forms of *oikodome* appear.

Building others up takes place when we work at maintaining peace and harmony in our fellowship (Rom. 14:19) and when we seek each others' welfare (Rom. 15:2). Loving others is essential if building up is to take place (1 Cor. 8:1). It is also essential to choose those things that are constructive rather than just permissible (1 Cor. 10:23, 24). We are also to share insights and understandings of God's ways with others (1 Cor. 14:3–18).

As we live together in love and unity, sharing ourselves fully with our brothers and sisters, we will contribute to the growth of individuals and the Christian community. Just as Nathaniel, hearing God's Voice in Scripture, set aside his concern for what he was seeking to build in this world, to build instead his own and his brother's inner spiritual life.

FOR REFLECTION

1. What would it mean if each Christian set aside his or her concern for building organizations or fortunes or reputations in this world, to concentrate on building up one another's inner spiritual life?

_____

_____

_____

2. Do you find your local church more concerned with building material things or more concerned with building lives? How can you measure the true concern of a local congregation?

_____

_____

_____

3. Nathaniel found that his concern over the land he had purchased was blocking his concern for the inner spiritual growth of a Christian brother. How often does concern for what we are building in this world conflict with our concern for the spiritual growth of a brother or sister?

_____

_____

_____

Before reading the next chapter, meditate on this article on Deuteronomy 6:4–7, from the Personal Growth™ Study Bible.

How do we help others come to know and love God? The family principles described here work in every relationship.

First, we're to love the Lord ourselves (6:4). Our own relationship with God comes first. Second, we're to take God's Word to heart daily (6:6). To lead others to

God we must be close to Him. Third, we're to build a family-type relationship with others (6:7). To lead others to God we must be close to them, too. Fourth, we're to relate God's Word to the experiences of life as we share those experiences with others (6:7). Others will come to know and love God if they sense His concern for the details of their daily lives.

LOSING YOUR "SELF"

*J*esus' teachings often puzzled His disciples. Many of the things He said puzzle us today. One of the most puzzling of Jesus' teachings is found in Matthew 16, closely following the report of Peter's confession, "You are the Christ, the Son of the living God."

Of course, those men who early on recognized who Jesus was should have paid the closest attention to what Christ said. And so should we, who also know Him as Lord. What Christ says may at times be puzzling. But we can never just pass over the hard sayings, shrugging our shoulders and murmuring, "Ah, well."

In fact, the words that Jesus spoke so soon after the disciple's confession of faith have tremendous import for anyone searching for the significance of his or her life. And they speak directly to our issue of fulfillment.

Here is what Jesus had to say to His disciples.

> If anyone desires to come after Me, let him deny himself, and take up his cross, and follow Me. For whoever desires to save his life will lose it, but whoever loses his life for My sake will find it. For what profit is it to a man if he gains the whole world, and loses his own soul? Or what will a man give in exchange for his soul?
>
> *Matthew 16:24–26*

In looking at these verses it's important to first understand the meaning of the word "soul" in Jesus' summary statement. Jesus is not talking about some immaterial human element. And when He speaks about losing one's soul, Jesus isn't speaking about eternal damnation. In Hebrew and Aramaic the word translated by the Greek word *psuche,* "soul," is *nephesh.* The *Expository Dictionary of Bible Words* (Zondervan) says that word means "personal existence. It is the life or self of an individual as marked by vital drives and desires. It is the seat of emotion and will. *Nephesh* is the 'I' of the individual, and is often used with the sense of a personal pronoun. Thus, while *nephesh* may mean 'life,' it is the unique personal life, the individual self, that is emphasized" (p. 575).

What Jesus is saying, then, is simply this. The person who is unwilling to deny himself, the individual who struggles to save his own life rather than lose that life for Christ's sake, will lose something utterly precious. He will lose himself. She will lose herself. Not the self he or she now is but the self that, by following Christ, he or she could have become.

How Karen Found Her Self

Remember Karen, whom we met in the first chapter? She was frustrated because the members of her small Bible study group seemed to ignore her needs. Like most of us, Karen had many personal needs she looked to others to meet. And it seemed only fair. After all, she had honestly tried hard to help the others. But they hadn't lived up to her expectations. As a result, Karen was feeling dissatisfied and cheated.

Then God spoke to Karen through Matthew 11:16–19. She read there about people who criticized John the Baptist for his austere approach to life. Then when Jesus came, enjoying social times with others, they were just as critical of Him. Karen wrote,

> *Here is a picture of a people who are never satisfied. They scheme and manipulate others for their selfish ends, yet nobody can ever provide what they really want.*
>
> *I was humbled to discover that this was an accurate description of many of my relationships. I often interact with people in ways that are designed to manipulate them to somehow meet my own needs. When they do not live up to these expectations, I become dissatisfied and feel cheated.*
>
> *The evening after God revealed this to me, I had my small group Bible study. I prayed that God would provide an opportunity to somehow apply the principles He was teaching me. I felt that this was a perfect opportunity because I had recently been feeling that the group had not been meeting my needs. I was not sure what that prayer would bring about, but I arrived at that evening's meeting with a different attitude. I went with a heart that was truly looking for opportunities to encourage, no matter what the cost to myself.*

What happened that night was not a major turning point in my life. However, I found many opportunities to simply encourage, to be vulnerable at times when I believed my experiences would be of benefit to another, and I did not hold back as I often do. I did not wait for others to meet my needs but actively searched out ways to become more deeply involved in their lives, regardless of their response. As a result, I left the meeting that night knowing that I had touched others' lives in a meaningful way and that I had truly offered a piece of myself. I felt more committed to and invested in their lives. And I felt more satisfied than I had in a long time. The satisfaction had come in giving myself, not in receiving.

A week later, one of the girls even told me that she had thought all week about one of the examples I had shared with her that night and that those words had significantly changed her walk with God. I was filled with gratitude that God had used me in such a way, a way that would not have been possible if I had been pursuing my own ends.

Several phrases in Karen's report of what happened to her have special significance.

"A heart that was truly looking for opportunities." Karen's approach to her relationships with the others in her Bible study changed. Instead of being concerned with what she could get out of the study, she went with a concern for what she could give.

"I actively searched out ways to become more deeply involved in their lives." Karen had been holding back, waiting for the others to focus their attention on her. Her attitude toward the others changed when she determined to take the initiative and see how she might be involved in their lives.

"I had truly offered a piece of myself." As Karen listened carefully to sense the needs others had, and tried to respond to those needs with whatever she had to offer, she found herself giving generously. She left that meeting knowing that she had touched others' lives. And, she said, "I felt more satisfied than I had in a long time." Karen discovered that satisfaction was found in giving, not in receiving.

"I was filled with gratitude that God had used me." Later Karen learned that God had used her to bring significant change in another girl's walk with the Lord. How thrilled and grateful she was. Suddenly she realized that she truly was an important person, whose life had meaning. God had used her, and her heart sang.

What had happened to Karen? As she denied herself, and focused on the needs of others, rather than on her needs a change took place. She lost the self that she had been—the self that felt dissatisfied and cheated—and she became the self that God intended her to be. The self that discovered joy in giving to others; the self that was filled with gratitude to God at the discovery that the Lord had used her to enrich another person's life.

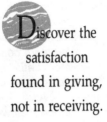

Discover the satisfaction found in giving, not in receiving.

Solomon's Meaningless Life

In Chapter four of this study guide we traced how, in Ecclesiastes, Solomon tried to prove to himself that he was significant. Like every human being, Solomon knew intuitively that he was important, at least to himself. Chapters 1 and 2 of Ecclesiastes tell us that when Solomon sought to experience his significance by satisfying his every need and desire, he became frustrated:

> I said in my heart, "Come now, I will test you with mirth; therefore enjoy pleasure"; but surely, this also was vanity."
>
> *Ecclesiastes 2:1*

> I searched in my heart how to gratify my flesh with wine.
>
> *Ecclesiastes 2:3*

> I also gathered for myself silver and gold and the special treasures of kings of the provinces.
>
> *Ecclesiastes 2:8*

> Whatever my eyes desired I did not keep from them. I did not withhold my heart from any pleasure.
>
> *Ecclesiastes 2:10*

But the more Solomon indulged himself, the more he concentrated on meeting his own needs, the less meaningful life seemed to be. And the more he felt not only unfulfilled, but insignificant.

And so Solomon searched desperately to find some philosophical proof that he was as significant as he felt, deep down, that he must be.

He looked at the patterns which exist in nature and the cycles that govern humankind's existence, and realized that these would go on repeating themselves endlessly, whether Solomon lived or died.

Solomon contemplated God, and realized that there was nothing he could do that would add to or detract from what God has planned. God existed, and would exist, whether Solomon lived or died, or even whether he had never been born.

Solomon considered the destiny of living creatures, and could find no sure proof that a human's destiny was any different from that of animals. Both suffer biological death, and how could Solomon know whether human beings continue to have a personal existence after they die?

Solomon looked at those relationships with others in which some expect to find meaning, and shook his head. Yes, it is better not to be alone. But there is no ultimate meaning to be found in binding yourself to a person who, like yourself, cannot affect the course of nature or the purposes of God, and who like yourself must soon die.

Try as he would, this man who had spent his life indulging himself could find no meaning for life at all. Vanity of vanities. Meaninglessness of meaninglessness. All, Solomon concluded, is meaningless.

Our Choice

What a difference in tone there is between what Karen wrote and what Solomon wrote. But there is more than a difference in tone. Solomon, committed to saving the life he has inherited as king, and committed to indulging himself, has in fact lost the self he might have become.

Karen made a choice to deny herself, and in the process she has begun to discover the self that she can become in Christ. In that process of discovery Karen has begun to realize that fulfillment is found in serving rather than being served. In giving rather than demanding to receive.

Jesus urged His disciples to deny themselves, to take up their cross, and to follow Him (16:24). Some Christians take allowing themselves no pleasures at all for self-denial. Others worry that if they like anything it must be wrong. But rightly understood, self-denial is living Jesus' kind of life in today's world. As Karen has begun to find out, that kind of life isn't painful, but rather is filled with joy.

But what about "take up [your] cross"? Doesn't the cross speak of suffering? Yes, but the cross is also a symbol of God's will. It was God's will for Jesus that He live His perfect life and die on the cross to pay for our sins. That is *not* God's will for you, or for me. But God does have a path He wants us to take, and good works He wants us to do. When we deny the selfish impulses that drive us to live selfishly, and instead choose to do God's will daily, we are following the path Jesus walked. And that path led Christ beyond the cross to an empty tomb, and to glory beyond anything we are able to imagine.

A little later Jesus spoke to His disciples about greatness in His kingdom. In a few brief words He sums up what it means to follow Him, and how we can do so. Here is what Jesus said.

Fulfillment is found in serving rather than being served. In giving rather than demanding to receive.

> You know that the rulers of the gentiles lord it over them, and those who are great exercise authority over them. Yet it shall not be so among you; but whoever desires to become great among you, let him be your servant. And whoever desires to be first among you, let him be your slave—just as the Son of Man did not come to be served, but to serve, and to give His life a ransom for many.
>
> *Matthew 20:25–28*

King Solomon chose to be served, and found life empty. Jesus chose to serve and give Himself for others, and He lived history's most significant life. If you and I would find fulfillment, we need to deny ourselves, and follow Him.

FOR REFLECTION

1. Have you had experiences like Karen's? Recall one or two, and describe how they made you feel about yourself and about the Lord.

_____

_____

_____

2. Explain each of the following phrases by illustrating from the life of Solomon and Karen.

    a) Deny yourself. _____

    b) Take up your cross. _____

    c) Follow Jesus. _____

    d) Lose your self. _____

    e) Find your self. _____

3. Because we are created in the image of God, each human being truly is significant. But we cannot live significant lives if we focus on the satisfaction of our needs. How does Matthew 20:25–28 relate to this truth?

_____

_____

_____

Before reading the next chapter, meditate on the following article on Matthew 16:24–26 from the Personal Growth™ *Study Bible.*

"If you like it, don't do it. If you hate it, it must be what God wants you to do." That's a strange notion, but one that has grown out of a misunderstanding of this passage.

In the New Testament the cross stands for Jesus' suffering, but it is also a symbol of God's will for our Lord. Jesus did not say we are to take up His cross, but our own crosses. We deny ourselves when our will conflicts with God's will and we, like Jesus, choose His will rather than our own. What happens when we follow Jesus in this? We lose the old life we lived, which was marred by selfishness, and we find a new life which Christ makes possible for us.

"Deny yourself" doesn't mean forcing ourselves to do the things we hate. It means discovering how to love the things God loves. Rightly understood, self-denial isn't deprivation, but delight. For the new life God wills for us is a life of purpose and joy.

STEPPING DOWN FROM THE THRONE

I remember the coronation of Queen Elizabeth. I remember it because the pastor of the little church I attended while in the Navy was a Canadian. What excitement there was in that home. They were going to watch it on television. They were going to actually see the coronation of "our queen."

I remember thinking how strange those words sounded to me. "Our queen." I didn't exactly laugh. But I did think it was rather funny.

Since then I've developed considerable sympathy for the British royals. I've often thought that the royal family is something like England's official pets. Most of the British have a great affection for their queen. But she herself is quite powerless. What a difficult life it must be, to be shown such formal respect by all, but not be allowed to even express her personal convictions about the issues that face her nation.

As the years have passed I've grown even more sympathetic. England's queen is one of the richest persons in the world. Yet she and her children have their days and nights scheduled years ahead of time. All that wealth, and they are unable to use it spontaneously, or break away to just do what they want. From all I've read, Elizabeth herself is a lovely Christian person. What anguish she must feel as the tabloids trumpet actions by her children that violate her most deeply held convictions. Elizabeth is a queen. But in so many ways that title is meaningless. She has no real ability to control the fate of her nation, her own schedule, or the choices of her children.

Yet, as we've seen, Solomon, whose royal position gave him unlimited power over others, felt powerless too. He was the most significant person in his kingdom, yet he was deeply aware that God alone holds the real power. That's a discovery many a self-made person has made after fighting his or her way to the top. A spouse demands a divorce, a doctor diagnoses a terminal disease, a loved one dies, an accident robs one of the ability to move one's limbs, and suddenly we realize how utterly powerless we really are. In the final analysis God alone is able to shape events to conform to His will. We simply cannot.

Another reason Solomon felt such frustration was that, no matter what orders he gave, they had to pass through a bureaucracy, where level after level of officials modified or ignored Solomon's intent. Solomon soon learned that the notion we can control others is, simply put, a fiction. That's something moms and dads learn too. We can set aside study time and insist our children read their schoolbooks. But there is nothing we can do to make them *learn*. The words, "But I did read it, Dad," often mean no more than "I ran my eyes over the words just like you told me to. Of course, I have no idea what the words *mean*."

> **G**od alone is able to shape events to conform to His will. We simply cannot.

Pressure to Control

One source of deep frustration in our lives is the fact that we often feel a need to control others. Often we do know best, but those we love seem determined to do things their way. Even when their way is the wrong way.

Liz, whom we met earlier, experienced that pressure in two ways. When Liz found Christ outside the church in which she had been brought up, her large family put all sorts of pressure on her in an attempt to control her choices. Her beloved father raged. Her brothers and sisters joined in the persecution. Although deeply hurt, Liz resisted the pressure and continued to follow Jesus in the way she felt was right. But how that pressure from her loved ones hurt.

Yet Liz felt just as great a need to control the members of her family as they did to control her. She looked at the doctrines of the church to which they had remained loyal, and asked herself, "How can they? How can they stay in a church that teaches *that*?" Liz began to feel more and more judgmental, and she subtly expressed her attitude toward her family at christenings and other religious events. Liz's attempts to control what her family members believed was less open than their attempts to control her, but her attempts were just as real.

And just as futile.

Liz refused to conform to her family's expectations. And her family refused to conform to hers.

Psychologists appropriately define conformity as "a change of behavior or belief toward a group as a result of real or imagined group pressure." The problem psychologists have, like the problem of worried parents and congregations of believers across the ages, is that there are two kinds of conformity. One kind is *compliance:* behaving outwardly as the group expects in order to be allowed to participate. The other kind is *commitment:* an inner, personal choice of the beliefs and values of the group. The problem is that from observing how a person acts, we can't tell whether he or she is conforming to be acceptable, or acting out of personal commitment.

How can we best help others develop a personal commitment to Christ and a Christian lifestyle, rather than merely pressure them into outward conformity?

We all understand this intuitively. Moms and dads realize it, and worry about how their children will act when they go off to college. Young people recognize it, and complain about hypocrites in church who act one way when all dressed up on Sunday, and act another way at home or on the job.

So we Christians need to ask an important question—and be sure we have the right answer. That question is, How can we best help others develop a personal commitment to Christ and a Christian lifestyle, rather than merely pressure them into outward conformity? How can we nurture an inner transformation; a transformation that is central to the growth of Christian commitment?

Liz began to learn the answer when she read what Jesus said in His Sermon on the Mount about judging. "Why do you look at the speck in your brother's eye, but do not consider the

plank in your own eye? Or how can you say to your brother,
'Let me remove the speck from your eye'; and look, a plank is
in your own eye? Hypocrite! First remove the plank from your
own eye, and then you will see clearly to remove the speck
from your brother's eye" (Matt. 7:3–5). Liz shared what this
passage taught her.

"It was easy for me to judge my family for choosing to
remain in a church that has teachings that run counter to the
Word of God, when they have all professed to know Him as
their personal Lord and Savior. It wasn't easy to look at the
attitude of my heart that they could see all too well. I felt the
Lord ripping out my demanding spirit, and teaching me to
rest quietly in Him and obey Him by acting in love when my
family persecutes me."

You'll remember that Liz soon had a chance to display her
changed attitude when she was invited to another christening.
"I was thankful for this new occasion where I could show love
to my family by being present at the ceremony, supporting my
brother and his wife as they dedicated their little girl to the
Lord. My heart felt right this time; I went with the energy to
"love" my family instead of "judge" them. I realize they are not
my enemies. I chose to pray, but not in an arrogant manner
this time. Through God's grace I was able to separate the
issues that cause me to react to persecution. There was still
some pain at the ceremony, but this time it wasn't self-
centered. My heart shifted to other-centered love as I focused
on their needs rather than my own hurt."

What happened here was that Liz gave up her attempts to
control the members of her family, and decided to accept and
love them as they were. This did not mean that she had to give
up her convictions. But it did mean that Liz had to show love
and acceptance, while permitting the others to live by the
convictions they now held.

Accepting Rather Than Controlling

When we human beings are left on our own, we quite
naturally feel pressured to control others. We want to climb up
on that throne, and make sure that our will is done. Sometimes
our desire to control others has an unhealthy source. We want

to control others so that we will feel important and significant. But it is also true that a strong desire to control others can grow out of pure motives. When we are guided by Christian convictions, we're even more sure that our way is right, and we can become desperate for others to adopt our ways.

The surprising thing is that God's Word insists we do the opposite of what our instincts tell us. Rather than pressure others in an attempt to control their beliefs or behavior, we are to accept them as they are, and *remove* the pressure. We are to extend to others the freedom to live by their convictions, not by ours!

The passage that develops this thought is Romans 14.

> Receive one who is weak in the faith, but not to disputes over doubtful things. For one believes he may eat all things, but he who is weak eats only vegetables. Let not him who eats despise him who does not eat, and let not him who does not eat judge him who eats; for God has received him.
>
> Who are you to judge another's servant? To his own master he stands or falls. Indeed, he will be made to stand, for God is able to make him stand.
>
> One person esteems one day above another; another esteems every day alike. Let each be fully convinced in his own mind. He who observes the day, observes it to the Lord; and he who does not observe the day, to the Lord he does not observe it. He who eats, eats to the Lord, for he gives God thanks; and he who does not eat, to the Lord he does not eat, and gives God thanks.
>
> For none of us lives to himself, and no one dies to himself. For if we live, we live to the Lord; and if we die, we die to the Lord. Therefore whether we live or die, we are the Lord's. For to this end Christ died and rose, and lived again, that He might be Lord of both the dead and the living.
>
> *Romans 14:1–9*

Several concepts in this passage give us direction.

"Receive" others. The word is a strong one. It indicates a warm, heartfelt, unconditional welcome. The believer is to not only permit others to join their meetings, but to welcome others into his or her life. This love is not only for the mature believer who understands the Christian faith and life as we do, but also for those who are "weak in the faith."

"Disputes over doubtful things." "Doubtful things" are matters over which Christians disagree. It's important to realize that this category is a broad one, including not only such matters as whether a believer should adopt a particular religious calendar or maintain a meatless diet, but even including the differences Liz has with her family over doctrine. A person is not saved because he or she does or does not speak in tongues, but because of a personal relationship with Jesus Christ.

There is another reason why "doubtful things" includes matters of doctrine. A new Christian may trust Christ as Savior, but never have considered whether or not the Bible is inerrant, whether evolution or creation explains the existence of the universe, or even whether Mary was a virgin when she gave birth to Jesus. We must give others the room to grow in their understanding, but demands that others conform tend to create resistance rather than encourage honest personal exploration.

In fact, the only issue on which the church is to take a stand against a believer is one in which a fellow Christian openly and unrepentantly adopts a lifestyle which the Bible clearly indicates is sin.

"Who are you to judge." All our attempts to control the beliefs or behavior of others involve judging. We not only must conclude in our own minds that what they do or believe is wrong. We must also conclude that it is wrong for them at their stage of development.

As a young Christian I joined a separatist church which viewed cigarette smoking as sin. When a young man who was a new Christian joined our fellowship, some of the young people wondered if it wasn't their duty to let him know that we viewed smoking as a sin. The pastor wisely said "No." He was able to observe what we did and didn't do. If and when the Lord spoke to him about his smoking he would stop. Until the Lord did speak to him, we weren't to judge him, but to love him.

"To this end Christ died and rose and lived again, that He might be Lord." This is the heart of Paul's teaching. Jesus is Lord. Christ suffered death on the cross, experienced resurrection, and lives today that *He* might be Lord. Jesus is no dead founder of the faith that bears His name. He has not committed control of His church or His children into the hands of any individual or ecclesiastical organization. Jesus is **Lord.**

Recognizing this reality we must surrender every pretense of a right to control others, and let Jesus be Lord in their lives as in ours. We can never find fulfillment, or significance, by trying to usurp a role that rightly belongs to Jesus alone.

How do we encourage others to grow in their relationship with Jesus, so that His lordship becomes the controlling factor in their lives? We acknowledge Jesus as Lord in our life, and seek always to please Him. And we accept others, even those with whom we differ, not to dispute with them or to judge them, but to love them for Jesus' sake.

FOR REFLECTION

1. What is one thing you believe deeply, and are troubled about because someone you love does not or will not adopt your convictions? How have you tried to influence that person to do what you believe is right?

_____
_____
_____

2. How does Liz's reaction to the "persecution" by her family illustrate one danger of trying to control others?

_____
_____
_____

3. How does Liz's attitude toward her family's decision to remain loyal to their church illustrate another danger of feeling a need to control others?

_____
_____
_____

4. Aside from the fact that we can't really control others, what does Romans 14 suggest about why we should not try to do so?

_____

_____

_____

Before reading the next chapter, meditate on the following article on Ephesians 4:15 from the Personal Growth™ Study Bible.

Have you ever noticed how some who are proud of being "truthful" are also cruel? Like the woman who devastatingly critiques a friend's outfit, and when the friend's hurt shows, says self-righteously, "I was only telling the truth." Or the upset parent who says to an underachieving child, "I'm so afraid you'll never amount to anything."

Scripture's exhortation to tell the truth is not license for cruelty, nor a reason to express our doubts rather than encourage. Ephesians 4:15 reminds us that we're to speak the truth "in love." We may think our friend's outfit does look terrible. And we may be really discouraged by our child's failures. But the truth must be spoken in love or it will harm rather than help.

Can't we ever criticize or rebuke another person? Of course. But we have to check our attitude when we do, and make sure that it's love rather than meanness or frustration that moves us. Only truth spoken in love is healing—and others *can* tell the difference.

GUIDANCE AVAILABLE

*O*ne of those fascinating insights provided so frequently by Scripture is found in Proverbs 14:12. "There is a way that seems right to a man, but its end is the way of death."

The average individual in any culture doesn't plan to sin. Certainly the Christian doesn't start out intending to do wrong. The pathway most of us choose is one that seems right to us. But there's a problem with our judgment. The path that seems right is one that may lead unexpectedly toward death, not toward life.

Nathaniel was doing what seemed right when he set out to establish his claim to all the land that he had purchased. He did the right things—he talked with neighbors, employed surveyors, called in the village elders. After all, he had a right to the land. He'd bought it and paid for it. Probably you and I would have taken the same steps, although perhaps not as patiently as Nathaniel.

Karen was doing what seemed right as she went to her Bible study. After all, she'd tried to be sensitive to others. They hadn't reciprocated. She felt hurt and unappreciated. It just wasn't fair. And so Karen held back, withdrawing emotionally. Certainly you and I would have felt the same way, and might have taken the same steps, although we might simply have stopped going to the group.

Liz was deeply hurt by her family's persecution. Not only was it unwarranted, they were wrong. All Liz wanted to do was follow Jesus, and her family had condemned and pressured her. What's more, Liz knew that *they* were in the wrong. It was their doctrines that were unsupported by Scripture, not hers! And so even though Liz kept on trying to love, she couldn't help judging her parents and her brothers and sisters. You and I would have done the same thing in our hearts, although we might not have hung in there for eighteen years, trying to love through the hurt we felt at family gatherings.

"There is a way *that seems* right to a man." We Christians try so hard to do the right things. Just as most people try to do what seems right to them. But then so often we realize that a way we've taken had led to death.

The steps Nathaniel took in trying to establish his ownership of the disputed land led to anger and hostility, and to the misuse of his pulpit. The steps Karen took as she struggled with her hurt and sense of unmet need led to greater frustration and withdrawal. The steps Liz took as she tried to influence her family led to estrangement and judging. Not one intended to do wrong. Not one set out intending to hurt or be hurt. Each set out to do what was right. But the way that seemed right to them led to disappointment and disaster.

Perhaps this is a good moment to stop and think about our own life. Is there a path we've been taking because it seems right, but has led to anger, or greater alienation, or judgmentalism? Is there a path we've been taking that seems right, but has begun to twist our attitude, deepened some division, or become a wedge between us and someone we love?

Most of us can identify some relationship, some situation, that troubles us. Like Nathaniel and Karen and Liz we've tried to do what seems right, but somehow the relationship or situation hasn't gotten better. If you're troubled by anything like this, now is a good time to stop and take a look at your own situation. Answering the questions that follow can begin a process that will bring you to a solution, just as the friends we've met in this book have found solutions.

If you feel uncertain about how to take these steps, use a separate sheet of paper and answer the questions as Nathaniel or Karen or Liz might have. After this practice, use the steps to help you think about a troubling relationship or situation of your own.

Identify: What relationship or situation troubles me?

_____
_____
_____
_____
_____
_____

Describe: What has happened in the relationship or situation?

_____

_____

_____

_____

_____

Explain: What have I done to try to repair the relationship or correct the situation?

_____

_____

_____

_____

_____

Evaluate: What impact have the steps I've taken had on the relationship or situation?

_____

_____

_____

_____

_____

The WORD, and a Word

Why do ways that seem right to us lead us astray? That's what Proverbs is telling us. "There is a way that seems right to a man, but its end is the way of death."

The reason leads us back to an understanding of the nature of sin. Some look at acts which the Bible labels "wrong" and think of sin simply as performing one or more of them. In Scripture wrong acts are sins, with a second "s." But sin, without that second "s" is something else again. "Sin" describes the impact of Adam's fall on the human race. "Sin" reminds us that we do wrong things because our nature itself has been warped and twisted.

Our emotions have been warped and twisted, so that we

often desire what we should not have. Our intellect has been twisted, so that the conclusions we reach are often mistaken. Our wills have been twisted, so that we often choose things that we know are wrong. What Proverbs 14:12 reminds us of is the fact that our judgment also has been warped and twisted, so that what we assume is right is often wrong, and acting on even our best judgment may lead to disaster. Nathaniel, Karen, and Liz each tried to do the right thing. But their judgment was flawed, and it took a Word from God to redirect them to the path that led to healing, and to personal fulfillment.

We understand that our only hope for peace here and beyond is to be found in a trust relationship with God.

The Word of God. You and I acknowledge Scripture as God's Word. We believe the Bible. We are fully convinced that its contents are not the pondering of religious men, but God's revelation to human beings.

The Bible unveils a reality which no human being can imagine. We are limited to what can be discovered by reason within the confines of time and space. God, standing outside of the material universe, can and has answered life's most basic questions. Through God's Word we know not just that He exists, but Who He is. We know His nature, His existence in three persons, His intent in creating, His motives in making human beings and His good plans for us as well as the destiny of our world.

Through God's Word we also understand ourselves. We find the explanation for our differences from the animal creation in God's gift to us of His own image. We understand our sense of right and wrong as His gift of conscience, the universal awareness that there is "something" beyond this life as something He has implanted in us. We understand our weaknesses and our tendency to do wrong as the expression of a sin whose origin Scripture explains. And we understand that our only hope for peace here and beyond is to be found in a trust relationship with God. And we understand why John sums up his Gospel by stating, "these are written that you may believe that Jesus is the Christ, the Son of God, and that believing you might have life in His name" (John 20:31).

As we explore the Scripture we find guidelines for living

our lives here and now. These are expressed as laws in the Old Testament, and as principles in the New Testament. Underlying both laws and principles is a revelation of the character of God. Both laws and principles flow from His essential nature as a loving, just, gracious, compassionate, forgiving, holy individual. The more we read and study our Bible, the more clearly we understand Him, and the better we understand Him the better we grasp the kind of life we are to live.

This is why Romans 12:2 reads "do not be conformed to this world, but be transformed by the renewing of your mind, that you may prove what is that good and acceptable and perfect will of God." The Greek word translated "mind" here is *nous*. In Greek and biblical thought *nous* is not so much the organ of understanding as the organ of perception. We experience transformation as the way we look at life's issues being transformed, and we come to understand God's way of dealing with situations and relationships. When we do understand God's way to respond to the challenges in our life, then we can prove— put to the test by experiencing—that God's will truly is good and acceptable and perfect.

Just as Nathaniel came to see himself and the dispute over land from God's perspective, acted on his renewed understanding, and found that God's will truly *was* good and acceptable and perfect—and fulfilling as well!

Just as Karen came to see herself and her sense of hurt as selfishness and a result of her own attempts at manipulation from God's perspective, acted on her renewed understanding to give of herself without expecting anything in return, and found that God's will truly *was* good and acceptable and perfect—and brought her a sense of fulfillment.

Just as Liz came to see herself and her judgmentalism from God's perspective, acted on her renewed understanding to love unconditionally, and found that God's will was good and acceptable and perfect—and brought her a sense of fulfillment.

No wonder the Bible says that "All Scripture is given by

When we do understand God's way to respond to the challenges in our life, then we can prove that God's will truly is good and acceptable and perfect.

inspiration of God, and is profitable for doctrine, for reproof, for correction, for instruction in righteousness, that the man of God may be complete, thoroughly equipped for every good work" (2 Tim. 3:16, 17).

A Word from God

Nathaniel, Karen, and Liz are students at Philadelphia College of Bible, in Langhorn, Pennsylvania. Each was enrolled in a summer class I taught there on the life of Christ, with emphasis on Christ's teachings on personal relationships.

As a pre-course assignment I asked each to read through Matthew and Luke three times, and to note passages in which His words or actions provided insights into personal relationships. Most important, however, was the assignment to select one passage that had personal relevance to them, put what Jesus taught into practice, and relate what happened. What you've been reading through this study guide are their stories, in their own words, which grew out of this simple assignment.

But there's something very important to note. Nathaniel, Karen, and Liz had been reading their Bibles for years. In fact, at school they were engaged in disciplined, regular study of Scripture. Probably a much more careful study than most Christians are ever able to undertake. Yet despite this, each of these relatively mature Christians took steps that seemed right to them—but which in fact led toward the death of their hopes and desires. Yet, when each went to Scripture with a specific question, with a desire to hear the Holy Spirit speak to them about one thing that troubled them, each one received a special, personal Word from God.

Most of us read the Bible as the Word of God. We need to learn to read the Bible *for a Word from God*.

When Nathaniel read the Bible for a Word from God, God spoke to him through Matthew 5. Nathaniel recognized his anger, confessed it as sin, and went to be reconciled with his brother.

He read.

God the Spirit spoke to him through the Word.

He confessed.

He obeyed.

He found peace and fulfillment.

When Karen read the Bible for a Word from God, God spoke to her through Matthew 11. She realized that she had been manipulating others rather than accepting them, confessed her sin, and set her heart to minister to others unselfishly rather than demand that they minister to her.

She read.

God the Spirit spoke to her through the Word.

She confessed.

Her attitude changed.

She found joy and personal significance.

When Liz read the Bible for a Word from God, God spoke to her through Matthew 7. She recognized her judgmental attitude, and realized that despite her hurt she needed to extend unconditional love to her family. She went to the next family christening with nothing but love in her heart.

She read.

God the Spirit spoke to her through the Word.

She confessed.

Her attitude changed.

She found joy and a sense of peace.

It really is important that you and I read and study the Bible as the Word of God. But when we're faced with a difficult decision, or concerned that a way we've chosen might not be the right way, we need to turn to Scripture for a Word from God. A very personal Word. A Word of specific guidance. A Word from God to you or me, which says "this is My way. Walk in it."

FOR REFLECTION

1. We're used to thinking of the Bible as God's Word. But are we used to going to Scripture seeking a Word from God? Is this even biblical? Check out Psalm 32:8, John 14:26, 1 Corinthians 2:12–14, Hebrews 7:1.

2. Before we are likely to hear a Word from God we need to come to Scripture with a clearer understanding of what we seek. That's why it can help to use a format like that provided in this chapter, in which we identify, describe, explain, and evaluate a situation in which we want to be sure of going God's way.

What is important is that after we have done so, we read the Bible expecting to hear a guiding Word from God. We can ask the Spirit of God to speak to us through the Word. And He will.

Before reading the next chapter, meditate on the following article on Hebrews 3:7—4:13 from the Personal Growth™ Study Bible.

God's Old Testament promise of rest has multiple meanings. For Israel, rest was possession of the Promised Land. But Israelites who failed to trust God disobeyed and could not enter His rest.

There is a rest for us, too. Ours, like theirs, is claimed by a trust in God which finds expression in obedience. In Creation God not only brought the universe into being, but from the beginning He solved every problem the future might hold. God is active today, but at rest. The labor of shaping the ages is done.

God knows us so perfectly that He discerns the invisible line that divides soul and spirit. God, from whom nothing is hidden, has given us His Word as our guide. As we look to God for guidance, trust His Word, and express our trust in obedience, God will lead us to the solutions to our problems that He worked out so long ago. And we will experience His rest.

BUILDING FOR ETERNITY

We began our study in search of a sense of fulfillment and personal significance. We met three people whose personal experiences were transformed by really hearing words spoken by Jesus Christ on a hillside some two thousand years ago. The words were unexpected, because they point to choices that seem unnatural to the average person. Instead of offering fulfillment, the words Jesus spoke seem to demand a surrender of self which, to the world, appears to bring the opposite of a fulfilling, meaningful life.

One book in the Bible helps here. It's a book written by Solomon after he had strayed from the Lord, and it described his personal attempt to find meaning in life on his own. Applying his marvelous powers of observation and reasoning, Solomon searched for meaning. His position enabled Solomon to travel every road that seems to most people to provide fulfillment and personal significance.

Solomon used his riches to enable him to develop his human potential. He designed and constructed great buildings. He created and organized successful businesses that brought him an unimaginable personal wealth. But when Solomon looked at what he had accomplished, he tasted ashes. Nothing he had built would last. Everything that he had achieved would crumble, and even the ruins would be forgotten. It was all meaningless.

In a sense, Nathaniel's experience recapitulated that of Solomon. He too is a builder. He doesn't have Solomon's resources, of course. But in his own way Nathaniel is a builder and entrepreneur. He found a way to come to America from Africa to develop his understanding and skills. He returned to use them in his home church. He found a way to buy land, to build a future for his family. Both his church and his land are important to this resourceful, ambitious young man.

Then came the conflict with his neighbor. At first Nathaniel focused on establishing his claim to the land. As the conflict intensified so did Nathaniel's emphasis on winning and holding what was rightly his. Even his ministry was subordinated to his drive to gain and hold that whole plot of land. Then God spoke and refocused Nathaniel's attention from his land to his brother. And Nathaniel set aside his concern with the material thing, which cannot last, and focused instead on healing the rift that the disagreement had caused. In making this decision, and in listening and acting on the Word he heard from God, Nathaniel became a people-builder, building not for time but for eternity.

Equipment for People-building

The structures that Solomon spent his life building fell into ruin. That's the destiny of every material thing in our universe. At history's end even what remains then will, in Peter's words, "pass away with a great noise, and the elements will melt with fervent heat; both the earth and the works that are in it will be burned up" (2 Pet. 3:10). Only one thing will remain when everything we've known in time has passed away.

People.

God, who planted eternity in our hearts, will not snuff out of existence a single human being. Each of us, self-conscious and aware, will go on being our individual self through the endless eons that lie ahead.

The thought is awesome. But it brings a special focus to our lives. The only thing that we can build which is truly lasting, the only achievement which has ultimate significance, involves our contribution to the spiritual birth, growth, and maturity of another person. Paul understood this truth completely, and reflected on it in 1 Thessalonians 2:19. He wrote, "For what is our hope, or joy, or crown of rejoicing? Is it not even you in the presence of our Lord Jesus Christ at His coming?"

When everything else has gone, we will find our fulfillment in that which we have built into the lives of our brothers and sisters.

When everything else has gone, we will find our fulfillment in that which we have built into the lives of our brothers and sisters.

Solomon was a builder. He had exceptional talents and gifts that were given him by God. You and I are builders too, and we are able to build people because of gifts God has given us. The Bible speaks of these gifts, which are called spiritual gifts, in three primary New Testament passages.

Gifts from the Spirit (1 Cor. 12). The first thing to realize about spiritual gifts is why they have that name. Our tools for people building are called "spiritual gifts" because (1) they are given by God's Holy Spirit, (2) they are tools of the Holy Spirit, and (3) they function to deepen and enrich the spiritual lives of believers.

Note what Paul says about them in 1 Corinthians 12:4–7, 11.

> God's Spirit works through us. It is His power which enables us to make a difference in others' lives.

> There are diversities of gifts, but the same Spirit. There are differences of ministries, but the same Lord. And there are diversities of activities, but it is the same God who works in all. But the manifestation of the Spirit is given to each one for the profit of all: . . .
>
> But one and the same Spirit works all these things, distributing to each one individually as He wills.

This brief paragraph establishes several basic points.

• Some special gift, some "manifestation of the spirit," is given to *every* believer. You are able to build in others' lives, for God has provided the enablement you need.

• Gifts differ, and you have your own special gift. Let's not envy another person's gifts, or assume that one gift is better, or more "spiritual," than another.

• God's Spirit works through us. His workings, like our gifts, will differ, but it is His power which enables us to make a difference in others' lives.

• Gifts are given "for the profit of all." God's special enabling gift has been provided to you so that you might benefit others.

What a significant passage this is. It tells us that each one of us is significant, not just because we are important to a God who loves us, but also because we can *accomplish important things!* We each have a spiritual gift from God. We can be builders!

The passage tells us that the Holy Spirit has chosen the particular way in which we will be able to help others. We don't have to envy others' gifts, or feel diminished because our gift is different. We can be builders!

The passage tells us that the Spirit Himself works within and through us. It is His enabling presence that makes it possible for us to contribute to others. We can be builders!

A context of love (Rom. 12). In the context of each major passage that speaks of spiritual gifts there is a stress on relationships. The context in which spiritual gifts are exercised is that of close, loving, personal relationships.

In Romans 12, Paul notes that God has shaped His church as a living body, in which each of us has a different function, just as the parts of our bodies have different functions. Each of us is to use our own unique spiritual gift to contribute to the growth of others. This leads to a series of exhortations, most of which urge us to establish and maintain loving relationships with others.

- Let love be without hypocrisy. (12:9)
- Be kindly affectionate to one another with brotherly love, in honor giving preference to one another. (12:10)
- Distributing to the needs of the saints, given to hospitality. (12:13)
- Bless those who persecute you; bless and do not curse. (12:14)
- Rejoice with those who rejoice, and weep with those who weep. (12:15)
- Be of the same mind toward one another. Do not set your mind on high things, but associate with the humble. (12:16)
- As much as depends on you, live peaceably with all men. (12:18)

Nathaniel's story illustrates that despite the fact that every step he took to resolve his land dispute seems reasonable and "right," each step drove a deeper wedge between him and his Christian neighbor. Then Nathaniel heard a Word from God, recognized his anger and confessed it as sin to God and to his brother. Suddenly the brother became more important to Nathaniel than the disputed half-acre.

The conflict had led to hard feelings in the heart of the neighbor as well. But Nathaniel's confession led to a breakthrough in the neighbor's attitude as well. He too confessed, and the two forgave each other. The breach was healed. With the personal relationship between the two reestablished, the dispute was quickly settled. But more important than that, Nathaniel writes "our fellowship grew, and our worship to God became whole."

With reconciliation came growth.

With love reestablished, God's Spirit could work without hindrance, and people-building again was taking place.

A blueprint to follow (Eph. 4). The same elements found in 1 Corinthians 12 and Romans 12 are found in Ephesians 4. God's gifts are given to equip believers for their work of ministry, for the edifying [building up] of the body of Christ (4:11, 12). Paul then goes on to describe what the completed building will look like.

> . . . for the edifying of the body of Christ, till we all come to the unity of the faith and of the knowledge of the Son of God, to a perfect man, to the measure of the stature of the fullness of Christ.
>
> *Ephesians 4:12, 13*

> . . . but, speaking the truth in love, [we] may grow up in all things into Him who is the head—Christ—from whom the whole body, joined and knit together by what every joint supplies, according to the effective working by which every part does its share, causes growth of the body for the edifying of itself in love.
>
> *Ephesians 4:15, 16*

God's goal is that each of us should become more and more like Jesus as we live our lives here on earth. And that transformation, worked by God's Holy Spirit, is something each of us contributes to as we use our spiritual gifts to build people.

What God is building is Christlike people, and this building of Christlikeness happens when each of us does our share, using our gifts in the context of loving personal relationships.

Discovering Your Gift

While it's special to realize that each of us has a spiritual gift, so that we can be people-builders, it can be frustrating if we don't know what our spiritual gift is, or how to exercise it.

So how do we discover our spiritual gift? Not by reading the New Testament lists and deciding which gift we'd like. Spiritual gifts are given for different kinds of service (1 Cor. 12:5). We discover gifts by loving and serving others. As we reach out to encourage, to help and support and pray, God begins to use us in ways for which we have been gifted. We do not discover our gift and then serve. We begin to serve, and our gift emerges.

What kinds of service are linked with spiritual gifts? Each New Testament passage in which spiritual gifts are dealt with is in a context that emphasizes close and loving personal relationships with other believers. Gifts are primarily interpersonal. Any context in which we build relationships with others and seek to serve them is a context for the operation of spiritual gifts. The context can be a Sunday school class. But the institutional setting (a church program) isn't necessary at all. We can minister just as well in a kitchen, in a small group meeting in a home, in a chat on the telephone. The necessary context is simply one of caring and serving others, giving what we have to enrich another's life.

How will we know our spiritual gifts? Our gifts emerge as we come to know and serve others. There will be three clear indications. (1) We find satisfaction in ministering in a particular way. (2) We see evidence that God is using us in others' lives. And (3) we find that others in the body of Christ sense how God is using us, and affirm our contribution. Then, when we better understand how God uses us to build people, we'll be able to focus our efforts on ministering in that way.

Real Fulfillment

Coming to the end of his life Solomon looked back on all his achievements and despaired. How meaningless the way he had spent his life seemed to be now. He had achieved so much. Yet in the last analysis he had achieved nothing.

You and I surely lack the gifts of intellect and creativity that Solomon possessed. But each of us has our own spiritual gifts from God. Each of us can minister to others in a way that builds them up, and helps them grow toward Christ's likeness. Unlike Solomon, if we commit ourselves to building people, we will be able to look back as we near the end of our life with a sense of real joy and accomplishment.

What we have built will last forever.

Our life will have been meaningful indeed.

And we will know what it means to be fulfilled.

FOR REFLECTION

1. We are each significant as persons God loves. But we can also become significant as people-builders. Is it enough for you to be significant in the first sense only? Why, or why not?

_____

_____

_____

2. For a time the land, a material possession, came between Nathaniel and his brother and blocked the process of people-building. Is there anything in your relationship with others that blocks you from giving yourself freely to people-building?

_____

_____

_____

3. Solomon could achieve only because God gifted him with wisdom. You and I can build people only because God's Spirit has gifted us for ministry. What about spiritual gifts in this chapter is most significant to you?

_____

_____

_____

4. Daily step: Take time to build your personal relationship with other believers.

Before reading the next chapter, meditate on the following article on Exodus 4:10–12 from the Personal Growth™ Study Bible.

We can understand Moses' feelings of inadequacy. Forty years before, Moses was consumed by dreams of delivering Israel. Now 80, having spent the last four decades as a shepherd, Moses has lost his fire. Moses knows now how foolish his dreams were, and has faced his limitations. He has no gift of oratory that will enable him to move others. He stumbles over his words, and struggles to think of the right thing to say. So Moses shakes his head, and begs God to find someone else.

Like Moses, we know how inadequate we are. When opportunities to minister come, we remain silent. When asked to teach, or lead a class, we draw back. We know our shortcomings. Find someone else.

But the God who said to Moses "I will be with your mouth and teach you what you shall say" is with us today. The wonder is that our shortcoming does not limit God, or limit His ability to use us today. So, God, don't look for someone else. Use me.

PUTTING OTHERS FIRST

Solomon was an important person. As the king in an absolute monarchy, Solomon was the most important person in the nation. But more than that, Solomon had a sense of his own significance as an individual.

Karen had a similar sense of her own importance. It wasn't just that her needs were important to her. There was more to it than that. Karen sensed intuitively that her needs were important in a larger, cosmic sense. She had a right to have her needs met because she was significant in and of herself.

Like Solomon and Karen, each of us grows up with a sense of personal significance. Our sense of our own worth may be crushed by abusive parents. Our sense of our own worth may be ground away by others who treat us as worthless. Or we may be coerced into surrendering our sense of self-worth by a spouse who demands the submission of every thought and desire to his or her own. But we all begin with the intuitive knowledge that we count. And that's appropriate. We do count. And because we count, our needs and our interests and our welfare count too.

> We all begin with the intuitive knowledge that we count.

A sense of our importance isn't wrong, because it is rooted in reality. God created us in His image, and we are important. We have worth and value as human beings. But our sense of our own importance can lead us astray.

> Our sense of our own importance can lead us astray.

Solomon reports that in his search for life's meaning he denied himself no pleasure. Anything he wanted, he bought or took. He indulged himself; he gave his own interest and needs first place. But despite the fact that he was in a position to satisfy every want and meet every real or imagined need, Solomon found life empty of meaning. His "me first" interpretation of the fact that he knew himself to be significant was a personal disaster.

Karen experienced the same thing. She writes of being nice to others in order to manipulate them to be supportive of her. Her "me first" interpretation of the fact that she knew her needs were important was a personal disaster too. When others did not respond as she intended, she felt dissatisfied and cheated. Her "me first" approach to relationships left her feeling unfulfilled and frustrated.

Then God spoke a Word to Karen, and she realized that her "me first" attitude was selfishness and sin. Yes, she is important. Yes, her needs count. But if she is important in and of herself, then the other people who she hoped would meet her needs must be important too. So Karen decided that she would deny her self, and seek to follow Jesus by serving others. She shared the result of that decision when she went to her Bible study group after praying that God would "cleanse me from my selfishness and help me to love others with a pure heart and a sincere desire for their welfare."

> *I found many opportunities to simply encourage, to be vulnerable at times when I believed my experiences would be of benefit to another, and I did not hold back as I often do. I did not wait for others to meet my needs, but actively searched out ways to become more deeply involved in their lives. . . . As a result, I left the meeting that night knowing that I had touched others' lives in a meaningful way and that I had truly offered a piece of myself. I felt more committed to and invested in their lives. And I felt more satisfied than I had in a long time.*

What Karen experienced was one of those strange and wonderful paradoxes of the Christian life. *We find fulfillment not in seeking to have our own needs met, but in seeking to meet the needs of others.*

This is what Jesus was talking about when He told His disciples that if they insisted on holding on to a "me first" attitude they would lose their true self. But in losing their lives for Jesus' sake, in surrendering their "me first" attitude to follow Jesus in serving others, they would gain their true selves.

In meeting the needs of others our need to become who
we are in Christ is met, our life becomes significant indeed,
and we find the fulfillment we seek.

Love and Putting Others First

One way that we put others first is by choosing to love
them. In our day "love" is a rather slippery word, with its most
common meaning in movies and music probably being, "to
satisfy our own desire by using another." In Scripture, however,
love is meeting another's need by choosing to act for their
benefit.

Probably the clearest single definition of love is found in
1 Corinthians 13. There the Bible says,

> Love suffers long and is kind; love does not envy; love
> does not parade itself, is not puffed up; does not behave
> rudely, does not seek its own, is not provoked, thinks no
> evil; does not rejoice in iniquity, but rejoices in the truth;
> bears all things, believes all things, hopes all things,
> endures all things. Love never fails.
>
> *1 Corinthians 13:4–8*

As Paul leads up to his description of love, he emphasizes
its importance. We may speak with the tongues of men and
angels, but if we have not love, Paul says, we've become
sounding brass or a clanging cymbal. Without love, "I am
nothing" (13:2). Without love, my ministry to others "profits
me nothing" (13:3).

The analogy is important. Love, that choice to put others
first which translates into the way we live with them, is
essential. Without it we are like "sounding brass" (13:1).

In the day that Paul wrote this letter there was a great
open amphitheater in Corinth. Near the back of the stage on
which the actors moved were large brass vessels, shaped like
giant vases. These were "sounding brass," hollow vessels
placed there to amplify the voices of the actors as they spoke
their lines. The sounding brass helped the audience hear the
dialogue. But the brass vessels themselves remained empty,
unaffected by the words that echoed from their mouths.

This, Paul says, is what happens to us when we use our gifts without love. Oh, we benefit others. God still is able to work through us. But the exercise of our gifts profits *us* nothing. We minister, but we remain empty and unfulfilled.

It's important as we contemplate this to remember that love is a choice, not an emotion or a feeling. Love is expressed in a decision like that of Karen, who prayed for help to love others and then went to her Bible study "with a heart that was truly look-ing for opportunities to encourage, no matter what the cost to myself."

As we reach out in love, God will use us in others' lives, and we will be fulfilled.

We can make this our prayer too.

And we can make Karen's decision to look for opportunities to serve others as well. No matter the cost to ourselves.

Then, as we reach out in love, God will use us in others' lives, and we will be fulfilled.

Love and Listening

Philippians 2 describes the attitude toward others that we are to nurture.

> Fulfill my joy by being like-minded, having the same love, being of one accord, of one mind. Let nothing be done through selfish ambition or conceit, but in lowliness of mind let each esteem others better than himself. Let each of you look out not only for his own interests, but also for the interests of others.
>
> *Philippians 2:2–4*

This image of other-centeredness rather than self-centeredness is a powerful one. For it to happen, we must know what's happening in others' lives. We need to know others' interests if we are to look out for them.

One of the most important things that a Christian can learn to do in a search for personal fulfillment is to learn to listen actively to others.

Books have been written on different kinds of listening. It's important, they say, because while 32% of our verbal communication involves talking, some 42% is listening. (Reading and writing accounts for the other 26%.) But there is one kind of listening that experts write about as really important. Some call it "social-serious" listening, by which they mean listening in an "informal, nonstructured communication setting." In plain speech, what that means is "conversation." Just talking together.

What makes just talking so important? It's the fact that to the Christian, other people are important. And good listening reflects our conviction that others count; that their interests and needs are significant. Good listening is a key to close, loving relationships. But good listening isn't easy, even when we truly believe others are important. Good listening calls for concentrated effort and the development of several skills.

What characterizes good listening?

Good listening is active. Sometimes when we're with others we focus on what we're going to say next, not on what they're saying. Active listening focuses on the other person. We listen not only for what is said, but for feelings. Tone of voice, a nervous laugh, a tightening of the lips, all can convey information about how a person feels about what he or she is saying. When we truly want to understand and when we care, we need to listen actively to what is said, and how it is said as well.

Good listening is reflective. Reflective listening means that we *respond* to the feelings others express as well as to the ideas they talk about. We reflect the feelings we think we hear. We don't reflect all the time, of course. But when a friend says, with her features reflecting stress, "Jim was late again last night," it's appropriate for us to say, "You sound concerned."

A reflective response may miss the mark. Our friend may not be concerned but rather hurt at Jim's thoughtlessness. But on target or off, our attempt to reflect her feelings is an invitation. It lets her know that we're willing to talk about that deeper, more significant "feeling" level of life that is so often ignored. We let her know that our desire isn't for a superficial friendship, but for a true, caring, supportive relationship.

Good listening is responsive. Caring relationships are never one-way. If we only listen actively and reflect feelings, and are always on the hearing end and never on the sharing end, others will become uncomfortable with us. Once we move beyond the superficial, we need to be willing to communicate our feelings and experiences as well as to hear these from others.

The whole process of sensitive listening is deeply imbedded in the Bible's description of how we are to live with one another. Caring, sharing, sensitivity, nonjudgmental acceptance, bearing of others' burdens, all these are woven through the New Testament's portrait of the Christian community.

No wonder then that Karen, who asked God to help her love, found herself at her Bible study listening actively to others, offering encouragement, and willing "to be vulnerable at times when I believed my experiences would be of benefit to another. . . ." She "actively searched out ways to become more deeply involved in [others'] lives."

In the process of losing her self, she found the self that God had created and gifted her to be. And Karen felt fulfilled.

A Loving Community

One of the most wonderful things about God's way is that it leads to life . . . for all.

We've seen that God's way to find your true self is to deny yourself for Jesus' sake. Solomon tried to find meaning in life by indulging himself and satisfying every passing desire. He ended up near despair, convinced that life has no meaning or purpose. In contrast, Karen, although deeply concerned about needs of her own that she felt were unmet, chose to set those needs aside and concentrate on loving others. She went to her Bible study group intent on meeting others' needs, and investing in their lives.

When Karen did, she discovered that she felt satisfied!

In giving she received.

In seeking to meet the needs of others her needs were met.

But there's even more to this way that God has marked out for us. God calls us to love, listen, and minister selflessly. But God calls our brothers and sisters to live the same kind of life!

Imagine it. Here is a whole community of Christians who put each other first! I am focused on the concerns of others. But at the same time the others are focused on my concerns! I let others know that they are important to me. But at the same time the others let me know that I am important to them! I invest myself in meeting the needs of others. But those same others invest themselves in meeting my needs.

And this is exactly what God has planned for us, and provided for us in one another. We are all important, and meeting our needs is important to the Lord. But our needs can be met, and we can find fulfillment in life, only as we walk in the way God has laid out for us, and put others first.

FOR REFLECTION

1. Why does focusing on our own needs and concerns to the extent that we put ourselves first in everything actually block the meeting of our needs?

_____

_____

_____

2. What difference might it make in your life if you prayed daily for grace to truly love others, and then looked for opportunities to encourage, no matter the cost to yourself?

_____

_____

_____

3. Do you have anyone who shows that you are important to him or her by truly listening to you? How important is that person to your spiritual growth and development?

_____

_____

_____

4. Try practicing the listening skills described in this chapter for one week. Then evaluate how they have affected your relationships with others.

_____

_____

_____

Before reading the next chapter, meditate on this article on Philippians 2:1–4, from the Personal Growth™ Study Bible.

The *American Heritage Encyclopedic Dictionary* defines ambition as, "1. an eager or strong desire to achieve success, distinction, fortune or the like; will to succeed." It also says, "2. A strong desire to achieve a particular end."

Ambition in the first sense is easily corrupted. A strong desire for success and personal distinction quickly becomes the "selfish ambition and conceit" of Philippians 2. But ambition in the second sense can be godly, depending on the particular end we seek to achieve. It will seem strange to some, but our ambition is to be like Christ in His humility.

When our ambition is to put others first, and to look out for their interests more eagerly than we look out for our own, our ambition is godly indeed.

STAYING OFF THE THRONE

*I*t was impossible for Solomon to get off the throne. He was hereditary ruler of Israel. It was his responsibility to rule. He was not only responsible to rule himself and his own passions, but also responsible to govern others.

Even so, Solomon found his role wearisome. Although he was king, and others showed him appropriate respect, Solomon came to the realization that his real influence was terribly limited. Nothing Solomon could do could affect or alter God's plans and purposes. The commands he gave that were intended to establish justice in his kingdom were thwarted by indifferent or venal officials in his bureaucracy. Even as an absolute ruler, Solomon discovered that he lacked the authority to impose his will on others.

It was terribly frustrating for Liz, who desperately wanted to influence her family members to follow Christ in the way she herself had chosen. It was frustrating for the family, who just as desperately wanted to force Liz back to their church. The family resorted to rage and persecution in an attempt to pressure Liz. But, as is usually the case, that kind of pressure failed to make Liz comply.

While Liz's attempts to influence her family members were more subtle (being outnumbered, she had less apparent power), they were nevertheless very real. Liz loved her family, but as time went on she found herself judging them, and her judgmental attitude showed through. And Liz's kind of pressure proved just as ineffective as her family's.

Letting Christ Be Lord

When we looked at Romans 14 in Chapter nine, we saw striking appeal. Scripture implores us to accept each other, welcoming one another as brothers and sisters. That welcome is to be real and wholehearted, with no disputing of "doubtful things." While we will disagree over matters on which

Scripture does not speak with absolute certainty, it is not our role to try to convince or change another's convictions.

Romans 14 reminds us that Jesus is Lord, and that each of us is responsible to Him. We are to place Jesus on the throne of our own heart, and in all that we do seek to please Him. And we are to resist trying to push Jesus off the throne of our brothers' and sisters' hearts by demanding that they do *anything* in an effort to please us.

For Liz's family to insist that she follow Jesus in their way, in their church, was wrong. But for Liz to judge her parents and siblings, even though convinced that in significant ways the church they love teaches erroneous doctrines, was also wrong. Liz, who acknowledges Christ as Lord in her life, simply had to let go and permit Christ to exercise His lordship in the lives of family members as well.

> It is not our role to try to convince or try to change another's convictions.

This is especially hard for us to do in at least two situations. First, when doctrine is involved. And the differences between Liz and her family were doctrinal as well as personal and emotional. We Christians rightly feel strongly about Truth, and so often feel an obligation to stand for Truth by trying to convince others whom we are sure are wrong.

Second, when long-term relationships are involved. It's so much easier to let go when we are not especially close to the others involved. In Liz's case, both she and her family members feared for each other. Each wants the best for loved ones, and each fears that the other will miss out on the best. Even when we know that we have no right to control another person, it's hard for us to resist trying to crawl up on the throne of a family member's life.

But there are passages of Scripture that help us let go in each of these two especially difficult situations.

Love and Truth

It's not surprising that the problem developed in the Corinthian church. This congregation that Paul founded was filled with highly gifted people—but was deeply troubled. In his first letter to the church at Corinth Paul deals with problem after problem: conflict in the church, failure to deal with immorality, marital problems, confusion over spiritual gifts, and so on.

One of the most troubling issues that divided Christians in Corinth had its roots in doctrine. On the surface it seems a silly argument to us. Some in Corinth thought it was really wrong to bring home a roast for supper. Others thought, "Hey, what's the big deal?"

The problem was that in that day meat markets were associated with pagan temples. The meat came from animals that had been sacrificed to idols. And that bothered a lot of Christians who'd been active pagans and had now turned their backs on the old ways to follow Christ. They didn't want anything to do with idols or idolatry, and the thought of eating even the most tender steak purchased from a temple market turned their stomachs.

What's more, they couldn't understand how any believer could even think of eating such meat! And before they knew it, these Corinthian Christians had slipped over the line and were scrambling up on the throne of their meat-eating brothers' lives! "No, No, No!" they cried. "You shouldn't! You mustn't! You can't!"

At first this amused the meat-eaters. Those members of the "don't eat meat" party were so immature spiritually. Didn't they know that an idol had no real existence? Didn't they realize that there was only one God? A Christian can shop at a temple meat market because he or she knows there's nothing to idolatry. How can a nonexistent "god" affect a person who knows and is committed to the true God?

But soon the meat-eaters found themselves feeling contempt for their "weaker" Christian brothers and sisters and more than a little resentment over the attacks the anti-meat party launched on their integrity.

Before long the division between the parties was wide and deep and marked by a growing hostility. Worse, each side appealed to doctrine to prove it was in the right.

"The Bible says 'no idolatry'! How can you!"
and
"The Bible says 'One God!' Idols mean nothing!"

And as long as the debate continued with each side appealing to doctrine to support its position, the division within the Corinthian fellowship grew.

So Paul in his letter to the Corinthians had to deal with this issue of a division rooted in doctrinal disagreement. He does so in 1 Corinthians 8—10. And he begins with a surprising argument.

> We know that we all have knowledge. Knowledge puffs up, but love edifies. If anyone thinks that he knows anything, he knows nothing yet as he ought to know. But if anyone loves God, this one is known by Him.
>
> *1 Corinthians 8:1-3*

The next word in the text is "therefore." Paul's whole three-chapter response to this problem of doctrinal division is rooted in principles he has stated in just three verses.

So what has Paul established?

We all have knowledge. You're both right! Idolatry is wrong. And idols have no real existence.

Knowledge puffs up. Trying to resolve the dispute by arguing over who is right has made you arrogant in your beliefs and intent on defending them.

He knows nothing as he ought. The problem with arguing Truth is that our grasp of Truth is incomplete. That is, while you are both right, you're also both wrong!

Love builds up. Try approaching your difference from the perspective of love. That will build you both up (edify you, help you grow spiritually).

If anyone loves God, this one is known by Him. If we help each other love God better, we'll be in fellowship with Him. And what this implies is that if we are in fellowship with the Lord, He can teach us both. With the Holy Spirit at work within us, whatever our present conviction, we can grow to know Him—and Truth—more perfectly.

This is what Liz discovered at last, and what she determined to do. She determined to approach her family without that attitude of judgmentalism which had created resentment. She was simply going to love them, and let Christ be Lord in their lives.

Now, this doesn't mean that Truth is unimportant. In fact, Paul goes on in the next chapters to develop several themes. He points out that love would move members of the meat-eating party to refrain from using the freedom they have to enjoy meat from temple markets in any situation where it might offend a brother whose convictions differ (chap. 9). Paul also dealt with an associated problem. If you're invited to a banquet at a pagan's home, go ahead and eat meat. But if your host makes a big deal out of the fact that the dinner and meat dish are in honor of some pagan deity, don't eat it as a testimony to the host of your commitment to Jesus (10:23–33).

And as far as "knowledge" is concerned, the "don't eat" party is closer to the truth (chap. 10). That's because idolatry has always been associated with immorality, and because real demonic beings are behind the deities pagans worship. It's best to have nothing to do with them.

But Paul concludes with another affirmation of freedom to live under the lordship of Christ. Each of us, "whether you eat or drink, or whatever you do, do all to the glory of God" (10:31).

Expecting the Best

It's wonderful to feel the freedom Christ gives us to love our brothers and sisters without feeling obligated to argue with them. But when we truly want the best for those we love most, it's hard to let go.

Here is a passage from Paul's second letter to Corinth which offers encouragement. Paul's explanation begins at 2 Corinthians 4:16–18. Despite the many problems in Corinth, Paul says "we do not lose heart." His reason is that "the things which are seen are temporary, but the things which are not seen are eternal." There may be problems now. But these are things he can see, which will change. What Paul is counting on is something that no one can see, eternal realities.

Without tracing his argument in detail, we can touch on the high points.

The love of Christ compels us (5:14). It is love for God which is the driving, motivating power for Christian growth and change. We are to count on Christ in the heart of our loved one to bring about the growth and change we yearn to see.

He died for all, that those who live should . . . live for Him (5:15). Jesus died to transform us as well as save us. It is unthinkable that Christ's great sacrifice would be in vain. God *will* accomplish His purpose in our lives.

If anyone is in Christ he is a new creation (5:17). When we come to know Christ God plants His own life within us. We are no longer left with only our own human resources. God, present in our lives, makes us new and different. Our hearts have been changed, and God will do the work within us that cost Christ His life.

> We are to count on Christ in the heart of our loved one to bring about the growth and change we yearn to see.

What Paul has laid out for us is a firm foundation for confidence that He will work in the loved ones about whom we are so concerned. But then Paul continues, to define our part.

> Now all things are of God, who has reconciled us to Himself through Jesus Christ, and has given us the ministry of reconciliation, that is, that God was in Christ, reconciling the world to Himself, not imputing their trespasses to them, and has committed to us the word of reconciliation.
>
> *2 Corinthians 5:18, 19*

That word reconciliation is critical. It means "to bring into harmony with." A good illustration is when we set our watch. We move the hands to bring them into harmony with the standard by which we measure time. Thus when Jesus died, it was with the purpose of moving us, that we might be and live in harmony with God, who is our Standard.

And now God has committed the ministry of reconciliation—the ministry of helping others come to the place where they and their lives are in harmony with Him. Of course, this is the very thing that so concerns Liz and many of us. We want our loved ones to change so they will live in closer harmony with the Lord. But what can we do?

What we do is to model our relationship with them on the pattern established by Jesus. In His great self-sacrificial act Christ chose not to "impute our trespasses to us." Rather than count our sins against us, Jesus reconciled the world by loving completely and giving Himself. And He counted on the love which the new birth plants in our hearts to work its wonderful transformation within.

Liz has learned the secret, whether or not she understands the principles found here in 2 Corinthians 5. She has chosen to love, to let Christ be Lord in her family members' lives, and not to impute their trespasses to them. In letting go Liz has found the way to peace and fulfillment. And the best way to bring her loved ones into fuller harmony with their common Lord.

FOR REFLECTION

1. Who is the person you'd most like to change? What does this chapter have to say about your relationship with him or her?

_____

_____

_____

2. What is the contribution of Romans 14 to our tendency to want to control or influence others?

_____

_____

_____

3. What is the contribution of 2 Corinthians 8—10 to our understanding of how to deal with those with whom we have doctrinal differences?

_____

_____

_____

4. What basis for confidence that God will work in loved ones' lives is found in 2 Corinthians 5?

_____

_____

_____

Meditate on the following article on Genesis 22:1–5 from the Personal Growth™ Study Bible.

"It'll be all right." These are words we resent. Lose your job, and someone says, "It'll be all right." The doctor tells you that you have cancer and the last thing you want to hear is, "It'll be all right."

We can imagine Abraham's horror when God asks him to offer Isaac as a sacrifice. Yet on the way to the place of sacrifice it's Abraham who reassures his servants. "The lad and I will go yonder and worship, and we will come back to you" (22:5). It's Abraham who says, "It will be all right"! How could he?

God had promised that Abraham's line would be carried on through Isaac. So Abraham was sure that even if God had to raise Isaac from the dead, the Lord would keep His promise.

That's how we can meet our challenges. We too can cling to God's promises and count on His love. In this way we can face uncertain tomorrows with hope, and affirm with Abraham, "It will be all right."

TEACHING PLAN

What Is Personal Growth?

To live healthy and happy lives we need to be growing in three important dimensions. We need to grow in our personal relationship with the Lord. We need to grow in our intimate relationships with others. And we need to grow within, developing a strength of character that will enable us to meet life's challenges successfully.

Personal Growth™ Study Guide Books

Personal Growth™ Study Guide books are intended to help believers grow in their relationship with God, their relationship with one another, and to strengthen Christian character. They teach foundation principles found in the Word of God and help believers apply them to daily life. These are essentially inspirational and practical books that major on personal application of God's Word.

This makes them ideal for use in a study group, whether the group meets Sunday mornings as a Sunday school class, or in homes as a Bible study. The Teaching Plan is designed to show a leader in any study group how to draw on the book and the group members' own personal experiences to have a truly significant learning experience.

Leading a Study Group

Some study groups have assigned teachers. Other study groups rotate leadership among members from week to week. Whatever approach you use in your group, the Teaching Plan is workable and easy to follow. One of the most important things to remember is that the leader of a study group is as much an *encourager* and *motivator* as an instructor. Because each member of the group will have the book you are studying, it isn't as necessary for the leader to teach content. The book provides the content, although the leader should be prepared each week to review key concepts for anyone who has not done the reading. As encourager and motivator, the leader will seek active participation by group members and encourage the kind of sharing that motivates members to put God's Word into practice.

A Simplified Teaching Plan

The Teaching Plan for each chapter is simple and easy to follow. The plan features:

Starter Activities:	These serve to open the hearts of group members to the truth explored. Starter activities usually involve participation.
Focus Activities:	These sharpen group members' understanding of the issue being explored and/or of a vital Personal Growth biblical principle.
Application Activities:	These help group members see how Personal Growth principles apply to life in general and to their lives in particular.
Sharing Activities:	These help group members motivate and encourage one another, pray for and support one another.

God bless you as you teach.

CHAPTER 1: ON OUR OWN

Materials Needed:
Books, Bibles
Chalkboard, chalk
Paper, envelopes

Starter Activities:
   1. Introduce yourself.
   2. Explain Personal Growth, and the role of *Personal Growth*™ *Study Guide* books (see above, or Preface).
   3. Invite other group members to introduce themselves, and suggest one way that some people try to find personal fulfillment. Each person should suggest a different way than was suggested before his or her turn to speak.

Focus Activities:

1. Divide into three groups. Give each group one of the following passages to read. Each group is to sum up what they see as personal applications of the passage. After fifteen minutes gather together again and ask for reports. The passages:

Matthew 5:21–26   Matthew 11:16–19   Matthew 7:3–5

2. Briefly comment on the significance of Jesus' promise of "blessing" for those who follow His hillside teachings, highlighting the three phrases developed in the text. Jesus promised a life of blessedness—of fulfillment—for those who seek it in living by His words.

Application Activities:

1. Depending on the time available, (a) read the stories of the three persons introduced in this chapter, (b) read one of their stories, or (c) simply tell group members that each of the passages they looked at has led individuals toward fulfillment, and encourage them to read their stories in Chapter one of the study guide.

2. Ask each to write on a sheet of 8½" x 11" sheet of paper: "Where I expect to find my own personal fulfillment." Also provide envelopes. Each person will place his paper inside an envelope, seal it, and write his or her name on the front. Explain that each will be given back his or her envelope after the course has ended, to see if and how his or her ideas have changed.

3. Distribute books, and assign Chapters one and two.

4. Close in prayer that God will give each of you a sense of personal significance and fulfillment as you each follow Him.

CHAPTER 2: LIFE WOULD BE BETTER IF . . .

Materials Needed:
Books, Bibles
Copy of questionnaire from Chapter two for each
Chalkboard, chalk

Starter Activities:

1. Distribute "My life would be better . . ." questionnaires. Have each person complete it. Then discuss each item together. How would each "if" affect your students' lives?

2. Then go back over the questionnaire, to discuss whether or not any can contribute to a sense of fulfillment. Why, or why not?

Focus Activities:

1. Read and discuss the first eleven verses of the Book of Ecclesiastes.

2. Discuss the fact that Solomon had everything found on the questionnaire, but was driven to the conclusion that life is meaningless. Why does this seem strange to most people? Why does it seem strange to us?

3. In a mini-lecture, review the distinctives of the Book of Ecclesiastes as developed in Chapter two of the textbook. Before doing so, underline in Ecclesiastes Solomon's references to "communing with his heart," and to search "by wisdom" and "under the sun."

Application Activities:

1. Place a vertical line divided into ten numbered segments on the chalkboard. Label it "Fulfilled." Have each person write on a slip of paper the number that represents his or her present level of fulfillment. Collect and place a check mark for each number by the appropriate segment of the line.

2. Distribute another slip of paper, and have your group members repeat. But this time write a number that represents the level of fulfillment that each expects to achieve at his or her life's end. Collect and also record.

Personal Growth Activities:

1. Invite any who wish to do so to share what is presently the most fulfilling thing in their lives.

2. Close in prayer asking God to use this study to enrich each group member's life.

3. Assign the reading of Chapter three before the next meeting.

CHAPTER 3: A LIFESTYLE OF THE RICH AND FAMOUS?

Materials Needed:
Books, Bibles
Chalkboard, chalk

Starter Activities:

1. Go around the group and have each member tell the most outrageous thing he or she would do if he or she won $24,000,000 at Lotto?

2. Go around the group again and have each member tell the most beneficial thing he or she would do with the winnings.

Focus Activities:

1. Discuss Solomon's use of his wealth. How did his use differ from the use of the "rich and famous" we read about in the tabloids or see on TV? Be specific.

2. Review just why Solomon concluded that even a wise use of vast wealth is unable to bring an individual a sense of fulfillment or personal significance. Which of the reasons Solomon advances, as discussed in Chapter three, seem most compelling to the group?

Personal Growth Activities:

1. Discuss: Based on individual spending habits, is there any indication that we are seeking fulfillment in possessions?

2. Discuss: The reading from the *Personal Growth™ Study Bible* raises an important question. What "advantages" do we want our children to have? Does our parenting suggest we expect our children to find fulfillment in things?

3. Assign the reading of Chapter four before the next meeting.

CHAPTER 4: ME FIRST

Materials Needed:
Books, Bibles
Chalkboard, chalk

Starter Activities:

1. Listening teams: Divide into teams of five. Ask each member to share one need he or she would love to have other Christians know about and respond to.

Focus Activities:

1. Discuss Karen's feelings about the group whose members seemed unconcerned with her needs (chap. one). Is it hard or easy for most Christians to identify with her? What

difference does it make that her needs were valid, and not merely superficial wants? Does Karen deserve to have her needs met? Do we? Why?

2. Mini-lecture: Solomon intuitively believed he was significant, and thus his needs had importance. But when he tried to prove that he and his life had significance, Solomon could not! Review Solomon's reasoning and his conclusion from the evidence.

Application Activities:

1. Discuss the article on Genesis 2:2 from the *Personal Growth™ Study Bible*. There is no evidence in nature of human significance. What about evidence in revelation? What other proofs of our significance can we find in Scripture beside the proof found in Creation? (For instance, we are important enough for Christ to die for, for God to want us to spend eternity with Him, etc.)

2. Discuss: If we truly are important, why doesn't it work for us to seek fulfillment in trying to find ways, or others, to meet our needs?

3. Pray, thanking God that each of the group truly is significant and important to Him.

4. Assign Chapter five of the text for the next group meeting.

CHAPTER 5: TOP OF THE HEAP

Materials Needed:
Books, Bibles
Chalkboard, chalk

Starter Activities:

1. Debate: Based on the ten things the author said he would do if he were in charge, have two group members debate the proposition: "The author of this book should be put in charge of the country."

2. Or, as a group, see if you can agree on ten things you would do if one of you was placed in charge.

Focus Activities:

1. Discuss. If the author (or your group) really were in charge, would it make any difference? Why or why not?

2. Mini-lecture: Solomon, who was in charge, became frustrated because he wasn't really able to make the difference he felt he should. Trace and explain his reasoning, as outlined in this chapter.

Personal Growth Activities:

1. Share: Who in your family or on your job frustrates you most? What would you do if you were in full control of their lives for just one week?

2. Share: Does someone in your family or on your job try to control you? How do his or her efforts make you feel? What does your reaction to an attempt by others to control suggest to you?

3. Invite group members to pray spontaneously for each other.

4. Assign Chapter six to be read before the next meeting. Point out that you are now moving to another section of the book. The first section explores the emptiness of the most common ways human beings search for fulfillment. This next section will look into Scripture to see God's guidelines for personal fulfillment.

CHAPTER 6: ETERNITY IN THE HEART

Materials Needed:
Books, Bibles
Chalkboard, chalk
"Points list" for each group member

Starter Activities:

1. Distribute a copy of the following "points list" to each group member. Have each check points which they do not quite understand or agree with.

Points in Chapter 6
1. God gives us capacities of mind, self-awareness, and moral awareness that are like His.
2. We can use the capacities God gives us to achieve in this world.
3. What we achieve in this world using capacities God gives us can never bring satisfaction or fulfillment.

4. Because God's gifts are spiritual, only achievements that have an eternal impact can truly satisfy or provide fulfillment.
5. We can't really tell how best to apply these gifts to achieve spiritual ends on our own.
6. God's guiding Voice comes to us through His Word to show us what to do.

Focus Activities:

1. Divide into teams. Let each group member choose his or her team based on whom he or she feels "most like," Nathaniel, Karen, or Liz.

2. Each team is to review the experience of its particular person, and answer these questions:

- Did what Nathaniel (or Karen, or Liz) do first seem reasonable? Why, or why not?
- Would what God directed him (or her) to do through His Word seem reasonable to most people? Why, or why not?
- What were the positive results of hearing and responding to God's Voice?

3. Reassemble the entire group, and hear reports from each team on what they discussed.

Personal Growth Activities:

1. Share a story about a time when you heard God's Voice guiding you.
2. Invite group members to tell of a time when God has spoken to them and shown them His way to deal with a problem situation or relationship.
3. Ask group members to pray spontaneously for sensitivity to God's Voice when they need guidance and direction.
4. Assign Chapter seven.

CHAPTER 7: BUILDING BIG AND BEAUTIFUL

Materials Needed:
Books, Bibles
Chalkboard, chalk

Starter Activities:

1. Write the following from Chapter seven on the chalkboard before class. Then discuss its significance.

> As long as the land had primary importance for Nathaniel, and his focus was on what he was trying to achieve in this world, he was frustrated, angry, and miserable.

2. Discuss: What seems to you to be the most significant differences between Solomon and Nathaniel? What do these differences suggest about our own search for fulfillment?

Focus Activities:

1. Mini-lecture: Briefly review the chapter, pointing out the differences in "building" achievements in this world and the kind of spirit-building "holy temple construction" that God has equipped us to do.

Application Activities:

1. Discuss: What would it mean if each Christian set aside his or her concern for building organizations or fortunes or reputations in this world, to concentrate on building up one another's inner spiritual life?

2. Discuss: Do you find your church more concerned with building material things or more concerned with building lives? How can you measure the true concern of a local congregation?

Personal Growth Activities:

1. Share: What is one thing that we can do to become better spirit-builders?

2. Commit: Invite each group member to share one thing he or she *will* do this coming week as a spirit-builder.

3. Pray for each other's building projects.

4. Assign the reading of Chapter eight.

CHAPTER 8: LOSING YOUR "SELF"

Materials Needed:
Books, Bibles
Chalk, chalkboard

Starter Activities:

1. Share: Recall the first time you ever heard or read Jesus' words about denying your self, taking up your cross, and following Jesus. Did these words seem more comforting or frightening?

2. Discuss: What did you think Jesus was asking for when you first heard those words? What did you think "self-denial" meant?

Focus Activities:

1. Together explain each of the following phrases by illustrating from the life of Solomon and Karen.

> • deny yourself
> • take up your cross
> • follow Jesus
> • lose your self
> • find your self.

2. Discuss what is wrong with this thinking: "Because I am significant, I deserve to have all my needs met and all my desires satisfied."

Application Activities:

1. Divide the chalkboard in two vertically. On one side write "Gentile rulers," and on the other side write "Great Christians."

Read Matthew 20:25–28 to the group. Together brainstorm as many contrasts and comparisons as you can find or that seem implied in this passage. List comparisons and contrasts in the two columns as they are suggested. Try to get at least twenty.

2. Looking at the chalkboard, discuss how this passage relates to Jesus' words about finding your self by losing your self.

Personal Growth Activities:

1. Share a time when you have found a sense of satisfaction in denying your self for Jesus' sake.

2. Incite others in the group to share their own personal experiences in this area.

3. Assign Chapter nine for next week.

Chapter 9: Stepping Down from the Throne

Materials Needed:
Books, Bibles
Chalkboard, chalk

Starter Activities:

1. Invite group members to define in a single sentence the difference between conformity and commitment.

2. Share: What is one thing you believe deeply, and are troubled about because someone you love does not or will not adopt your convictions? How have you tried to influence that person to do what you believe is right? Has it worked?

Focus Activities:

1. Have each person read and mark Romans 14:1—15:6, as follows:

> • <u>Underline</u> what seem to be key verses.
> • Box verses that tell you what to do.
> • Place a "question mark" beside any verse you do not understand.

2. Break into teams of four or five to study and discuss Romans 14:1—15:6. Do this by comparing what each of you underlined, boxed, or questioned.

3. After 15 to 20 minutes reassemble, and discuss any questions team members raised that were not answered.

Application Activities:

1. Discuss: What dangers of trying to control others rather than accept them does Liz's experience illustrate?

2. Discuss: What would it mean for others to let Christ be Lord in your life? What would it mean for you to let Christ be Lord in a loved one's life?

Personal Growth Activities:

1. Share: Who in your experience has modeled Christian acceptance toward you? What does that person mean to you? Has he or she contributed to your growth as a person and a Christian? How?

2. Invite sponaneous prayer about developing and expressing an accepting attitude.

3. Explain that you are now approaching the third section in this study of fulfillment. Each chapter in this section contains specific ideas on how to find fulfillment by practicing the principles of listening for God's Voice, giving priority to people-building, putting others first, and letting Christ be Lord in others' lives.

4. Assign Chapter ten. Encourage each group member to read the chapter early, and put into practice its guidelines during the week before your next meeting.

CHAPTER 10: GUIDANCE AVAILABLE

Materials Needed:
Books, Bibles
Chalkboard, chalk
3 Worksheets (pages 74, 75) for each member
Tables, pens, pencils

Starter Activities:
1. Have each select Nathaniel, Karen, or Liz, and fill out one of the worksheets as he or she might have. Complete each segment: What troubled me? What happened? What have I done to try to repair or correct? What has been the impact of the steps I've taken?

Encourage each person to do a careful, thorough job. Members can refer to the textbook for help if they wish.

2. Use the chalkboard to summarize the worksheet results on each person. Let group members who have worked on an individual's situation contribute to the composite.

Focus Activities:
1. Mini-lecture: Describe "general" study of Scripture, in which a person reads the Bible as the Word of God, to better understand God and His ways. Then describe a "specific" study of Scripture, what the author calls reading "for a Word from God."

Illustrate from the experiences of Nathaniel, Karen, and Liz how that Word from God has guided them to deal correctly with the situations you have just described on worksheets.

2. Invite group members to tell of a time when God has given them a guiding Word through Scripture.

Application Activities:

1. Give each group member another worksheet. Ask each to complete it, analyzing a particular relationship or situation that troubles them at this time.

2. In teams of four or five read worksheets to each other. Have the others respond by suggesting passages of Scripture that might be relevant, which the reader can check out.

3. After each person in a team has had a chance to share, close in teams, pray for each other.

4. Assign Chapter eleven for the next group meeting. Give each person another worksheet to use in the future. Encourage them to read God's Word this coming week for a Word from God which will give specific guidance for the situation described in class on the worksheet.

CHAPTER 11: BUILDING FOR ETERNITY

Materials Needed:
Books, Bibles
Chalkboard, chalk

Starter Activities:

1. Invite individuals to share any Word from God they have received this past week.

2. Write on the chalkboard, "We find fulfillment in building others up."

3. Go around the group and briefly talk about the person who has been most significant in building each person up as a Christian.

Focus Activities:

1. Draw five horizontal lines on the chalkboard. Each line represents a continuum, the whole range from one end of the spectrum to the other. Ask each group member to mentally place check marks along each line where it best describes their relationship with the person most significant in building them up.

Close ⎯⎯⎯⎯⎯⎯⎯⎯⎯⎯⎯⎯⎯⎯	Distant
one-way ⎯⎯⎯⎯⎯⎯⎯⎯⎯⎯⎯⎯	two-way
Warm ⎯⎯⎯⎯⎯⎯⎯⎯⎯⎯⎯⎯⎯	Formal
knew me personally ⎯⎯⎯⎯⎯⎯⎯⎯⎯⎯⎯⎯⎯⎯	did not know personally
knew him/her well ⎯⎯⎯⎯⎯⎯⎯⎯⎯⎯⎯⎯	did not know well

2. Divide each line into four equal segments. Have group members raise hands to indicate where their check marks went. (You will find that nearly all check marks will be in the first or second quarter to the left of the line!)

3. The author pointed out in Chapter eleven that people-building spiritual gifts operate in a context of love. Discuss: How does our own experience reflect what the Bible passages on gifts teach?

Application Ideas:

1. Daily step. The author suggests that the most important thing we can do as people-builders is to deepen our relationships with others. Discuss in general how to deepen relationships. Discuss specifically how you can grow closer as members of your Bible study group. Then ask each to plan one thing he or she will do to deepen one relationship.

2. If your group members have come to know each other significantly, pick one person. Other group members will share how he or she has contributed to their lives. When all who wish have shared, pick another, and continue the process. This activity may help individuals learn more about their spiritual gift and encourage them to exercise it.

3. Pray spontaneously, thanking God for individuals who have contributed to personal spiritual growth.

4. Assign Chapter twelve.

CHAPTER 12: PUTTING OTHERS FIRST

Materials Needed:
Books, Bibles
Chalkboard, chalk
Information on other *Personal Growth*™ *Study Guides*

Starter Activities:

    1. Write on the chalkboard, "We find fulfillment in putting others first."

    2. Review Jesus' words in Matthew 16 on denying oneself and saving oneself (see Chapter eight). Make sure everyone understands what this passage is teaching.

Focus Activities:

    1. Read what Karen wrote, as quoted on page 90. Discuss: How did she deny herself? What did she gain?

    2. Mini-lecture: Remind the group that there is sick as well as healthy self-denial. Sick self-denial will be characterized by:

        a) A selfish, hidden motive. We deny our wants for our own sake.

        b) A sense of personal worthlessness.

        c) An inner resentment.

Healthy self-denial, in contrast, is characterized by:

        a) A love for others. We deny our wants for Jesus' sake.

        b) A sense of personal worth and value.

        c) An inner satisfaction.

Point out that it is important not to confuse sick and healthy self-denial, and review what the chapter says about "love."

Personal Growth Activities:

    1. Divide into teams of three. Invite each individual to share one situation or relationship that troubles him or her now, while the others listen actively, reflectively, and responsively.

    2. After each has had a chance to share and be heard, pray in teams of three for each other.

    3. Reassemble. Go around the circle and give each person a chance to share one thing that he or she has gained from your study together these past weeks.

    4. Assign Chapter thirteen. You may wish to discuss starting another *Personal Growth* study together.

CHAPTER 13: STAYING OFF THE THRONE

Materials Needed:
Books, Bibles
Chalkboard, chalk

Starter Activities:

1. Write on the chalkboard, "We find fulfillment in giving others freedom to let Jesus be Lord."

2. Discuss: When is it hardest for you to "let go" and give others the freedom to make their own choices?

3. Share: Who is the person you'd most like to change? What does this chapter suggest about your relationship with him or her?

Focus Activities:

1. Mini-lecture: Review the teaching of Romans 14, as developed earlier in Chapter nine.

2. Open Bibles to 1 Corinthians 8—10. Think through 8:1-4 together. Then see if group members have questions or comments on the rest of these chapters. (Note that "eating meat" is also mentioned in Romans 14. This issue must have been important throughout the early church.)

3. Open Bibles to 2 Corinthians 4, 5, and examine the verses that the author comments on.

Application Ideas:

1. Discuss: How does it make us feel to know that God is at work, and will work, in the lives of those we love but are concerned for?

Culminating Activity:

1. You may wish to review the entire study, to put everything in perspective. Simply: On our own, we do not know what brings fulfillment. Human beings use their God-given gifts and abilities to achieve worldly goals which can never truly satisfy. Only God, who has placed eternity in our hearts, can show us how to find fulfillment. We actually find fulfillment in building people, in putting others first, and in resisting taking Christ's lordship role in others' lives. In the last section of the book we focused on developing the skills and attitudes that would bring us fulfillment.

2. If time permits, let members share the most important contribution this group study has made to their lives.